T0083939

PRIVATE LESSONS

The Complete Guide

by Henry Soleh Brewer

ISBN-13: 978-1-4234-1250-2
ISBN-10: 1-4234-1250-8

HAL•LEONARD®
CORPORATION
7777 W. BLUEMOUND RD. P.O. BOX 13819 MILWAUKEE, WI 53213

In Australia Contact:
Hal Leonard Australia Pty. Ltd.
4 Lentara Court
Cheltenham, Victoria, 3192 Australia
Email: ausadmin@halleonard.com

Visit Hal Leonard Online at
www.halleonard.com

About the Author

Henry Soleh Brewer studied music at Webster University Conservatory in St. Louis, Missouri. He went on to play with such greats as B.B. King, the O'Jays, the Emotions, and members of Earth, Wind & Fire. Henry is also a songwriter/producer and has recorded keyboards on radio jingles, television commercials, and the films *Police Academy 2*, *Bob Roberts*, *Nemesis*, *Fast Getaway 2*, and more. In 1990 Henry became one of the founding keyboard instructors at Musicians Institute's Keyboard Institute of Technology in Hollywood, California.

During the '90s, Henry performed keyboards for Earth, Wind & Fire's Hall of Fame bassist Verdine White, on his instructional video for bass. Henry has written several books and has performed on several instructional CDs and videos, including two of his own Blues keyboards instructional DVDs for Warner Brothers/ DCI. Henry wrote the heralded *R&B Soul Keyboards* book in 1999, and co-authored *Pop Rock Keyboards* along with David Garfield in 2005, both for Hal Leonard Corporation. Currently, Henry is collaborating with Earth, Wind & Fire drummer Fred White on an upcoming CD project. He continues to teach various classes and private lessons at Musicians Institute.

For additional information, visit **solehbrewer.com**.

About the CD and Artist Credits

All tracks were created on the Korg Triton Workstation and the Yamaha Motif 6 Workstation, and were recorded using Pro Tools. Each track plays the musical example first with keyboards, then once again, minus keyboard parts so you can play along.

> Keyboards and Drum Programming: Henry Soleh Brewer
> Additional Programming: Chuck Jefferson
> Notation: Rachel Yoon and Henry Soleh Brewer
> Sample and Wave Graphics: Gary Solt
> Engineer: James Rhee

Although Hip-Hop is commonly filled with samples and loops, it may serve the readers better to provide re-created MIDI tracks. This was done in order to encourage the potential player to use common sounds found on these types of keyboards, enabling him/her to play along with the arrangements in this book. By finding these sounds on your own workstations, you will eventually learn how to create within the Hip-Hop environment.

The examples have been composed with even numbers of measures so the reader may record them to use as samples and loops with respect to practicing the exercises in this book. Any pattern that becomes looped can then be practiced repetitively for continuity, and to establish a groove.

Acknowledgements

I would like to dedicate this book to my daughter Angel Wade Brewer. I wish you love, prosperity, and health. Anchk, Uja Seneb! Thanks for all of your great Hip-Hop dance expertise and especially the vital information. I send all my love and heartfelt thanks to you, Isis Cheryl Wade Brewer, my love and partner. You are always there for me and I am eternally grateful! To my mother Deborah Brewer, I will always love and cherish you, much happiness. Thanks to my sister Cleazel Brewer and my brother John Brewer. Special thanks to the entire Wade family from St. Louis. Special thanks to Sekou Olatunji, my other brother. Thanks, Kenny Rogers, for your tireless support and special trip you took all the way from the east coast; you are my brother! Special thanks to Morris Hunter and family. Thank you, brother Greg Happy Haynes (represent from the Lu), for your many talents and gifts, and for your generosity. To all my family and close friends, I am sending positive vibes of success, prosperity, life, and wisdom.

To my departed friend, the great Louis Satterfield, I bid farewell for the time being but we shall live and laugh again on a higher plane. Thanks for all of your support, talent and especially your pioneering spirit. Vibrations! Asante, Keith, DaMia and Yuba Satterfield and family. To Woody Washington, Emzee, Jimmy Smith, Lou Rawls, Ray Charles, King Floyd, Claydes Charles Smith, Milan Williams, Gerald Levert, James Brown, and Billy Preston with respect, I bid "Ohmm" to the power and glory! We will always love you!

I'd like to thank you, Freddie White, for your continued support and encouragement. We are joined at the hip, for life. You are my brother. Larry Dunn, you know what you mean to me! You are all that I want to be and more—you are my brother, and thanks for sharing him, Luisa. Special thanks to you Masta, you are the essence of the creator. Thanks for everything—you are my brother. Thanks Patrice Rushen for your friendship, inspiration, and spirit. Your talents have no limits—you are my sister, and blessings to your entire family. Thank you, Gail Johnson, you are a great talent and I feel blessed to work with you. You are my sister!

Thank you, Alan Abrahams and Margaret Fowler Abrahams, for all the great times in the studio, the food and the music. There's nothing better than that, is there? Thanks, Paul Jackson, Jr., you are the man! It is always a blessing from the creator to work with you…hope you enjoyed the *Pop Rock Keyboards* book! Thanks, Ren Woods, for your words of encouragement, and thanks, Katerina Graham and Cedric the Entertainer, for working with me on the great songwriting project. Let's make some hits!

Thanks to everyone at Hal Leonard Corporation.

Thanks to all of the talented staff at Musicians Institute. Special thanks to Fred Dinkins, Chuck Jefferson, Eric, Bubba Bryant, Tom Whitt, Tio Banks, Masta, Jamie Findley, Carlos Campos, Chas Grasamke, Roger Steinman, Kevin King, Chuck Silverman, Cho, Alby Dunbar, Carol Rogers, Lupo, David Valencia, Mike Campbell, Jim McMains, Rick Zunigar, Greg Poree, Maurice Verloop, Fred Dinkins, Keith Wyatt, Norman Brown, Coco, Marie, Deena, Coreen, Tim, and Tita, and all of you guys who have offered me kind words, support, and encouragement. It really means a lot!

Rachael Yoon, Chuck, Masta, Kenny Rogers, Sekou Olatunji, Al Perkins, Jr., Angel Wade, Jeff Chang, Dr. Kweku Person-Lynn, Danny Diaz, Dave Dunkerly, James Rhee, and Gary Solt: thank you for all the insightful contributions that went into the making of this book. It's been a pleasure working with you.

Lastly, I would like to thank Jerry Kovarsky at Korg Inc.

Preface

This book is designed as a guide and method book for aspiring Hip-Hop keyboard players. There are many facets to playing a keyboard within this style of music that remain unexplored and unexplained. Throughout the music instruction world, strides are being made toward attempting to bring this art form to the forefront. Many books and videos are being created on the topics of sequencing, sampling, turntable operation/DJ, drum programming, production, arranging, and playing live in Hip-Hop bands. Most of these books and videos are created by young budding artists/producers and many are directed at non-musicians. If these books are directed at musicians at all, then they are usually for guitarists, bass players or drummers.

Never before has an experienced keyboard player created a complete method book that focuses on all of the related aspects of becoming a contemporary Hip-Hop keyboard player. This book has been written for musicians who play other styles and are interested in learning the tenets of this ever-expanding prevailing genre. This book will also serve as a reference for all those interested in exploring the sounds, rhythms, and influences that go into the makings of rap and Hip-Hop recordings.

In this book we will explore the history of this music as demonstrated with audio examples provided on CD. The history of rap music, from its inception in the late '70s through Hip-Hop's origins in the '80s, has changed music as we know it. This music has expanded over the past twenty-five years and has become a mainstay in popular music, and its influence is currently heard, seen, and felt throughout the world. In order to fully grasp the role of the keyboard player in all of this, we will take an in-depth look at the early songs, producers, and musicians who helped to bring this style to life. Included will be musical examples that chronicle the works of early rap recordings (Sugarhill Gang, Doug E. Fresh, J.J. Fad, LL Cool J, etc.). These examples will progress throughout the book, into Hip-Hop songs, producers, and musicians (Full Force, Teddy Riley, Jelly Bean Benitez, etc.).

Once the Hip-Hop examples are introduced historically, the examples will branch off to detail more contemporary songs, artists, and producers (Dr. Dre, Eminem, Timbaland, Pharrell, Missy Elliott, P Diddy Combs, Kanye West, etc.).

There are ten chapters which contain information and examples that should progress the student toward more difficult information and tasks. In addition to the CD examples, musical notation of the keyboard parts is included to acquaint you with some of the most common patterns and techniques you will need in order to play off the *heezie* for *sheezie* my *neezie*. Each chapter contains five to eight examples for students to work with. Listening tips are also provided to help the student understand the genre. In some cases, illustrations have been employed to help the student further understand their connection with the music. A list of reference materials and resources, and a list of contemporary rap and Hip-Hop keyboard players are also included for further study. So take your time, listen closely to each exercise, examine the notation thoroughly, practice, and most of all, open up to the attitudes and feel in the music, and get your groove on 4 sho'.

PEACE

Henry Soleh Brewer

Contents

Introduction

Hip-Hop music is now an internationally accepted style of music finding common ground amongst the world's many cultures! It has become one of the world's greatest and most popular styles of music at this present date. The growth of its record sales has reached new industry heights within a relatively short amount of time, grossing millions upon millions of dollars. Hip-Hop music is known worldwide for its powerful grooves, its hypnotic rhythms, unique harmonic resonance, and its infectious style and flavor.

This music makes the entire world want to move and dance with swagger and grace. Hip-Hop has messages of hope to the youth; it shares and lends direction to the lost. It provides confidence to the timid and confused, and brings startling new and uncharted vision to those who are searching for a better way. Hip-Hop has become a way for the older folks who have grown weary of the message of the older generation to find new meaning and new ways of expressing ethnic ideas. Hip-Hop is a language all by itself, but it has not always been this way.

Like the blues, Hip-Hop started on a rugged and bumpy road. The infant face of Hip-Hop was scarred and tainted by a society that did not want to hear from the originators of this music. The societal ear of Hip-Hop was far from being open. Racial stereotypes, social barriers, and down right disdain for the originators of this music prevailed. Many people, young and old, who consider themselves singers, artists, teachers, and laypersons alike, to this very day, do not consider rap or Hip-Hop music at all. Even the author of this book once considered it a nonmusical fad that would run its course within a few years. We will explore the real ideas behind this music and really take a look and listen to its pros and cons. We will examine this music thoroughly and gain some access into a world that has grown beyond America's borders.

Hip-Hop found its origins in the raw uncut beats of the Black youth. This idea, as true with all music genres, is one that is a result of the culture, lifestyle, fashion, and events of that period of time. It is a direct result of racial identity and self-pride. However misguided and misunderstood rap has been accused of being, the music became a way of validating its artists in the midst of public and societal ridicule. So Hip-Hop and rap must go hand in hand in order to relate to the direction and tenets of the music. In order to understand Hip-Hop you must look into the origins of rap music.

Rap music is a roots style within African traditions that developed over many, many years. Its influence can be heard in early drum and vocal chants by griots during ritual ceremonies and celebrations. Rap music has been a consistent ingredient within many African American musical genres. Rap (Rhythmically Applied Poetry) began picking up steam from the early days of minstrel music and R&B (1940s), and was featured in many R&B/funk songs of the late 1970s. In the early 1980s, rap came on the scene as an exclusive musical genre.

Rap music is the musical foundation of Hip-Hop, but Hip-Hop contains elements that are more advanced than rap music and thus creates a difference. The musical accompaniments for rappers were grooves literally borrowed from existing R&B hit songs. In many cases, the songs were lifted without permission. This became the prototype formula for rap music, and the rhythms and harmonies were purposely left simple. However, solid backbeats and simple catchy bass lines and melodies gave the music character. This left plenty of space for the rappers to supply creative rhythms that would add bounce and life (hip and hop) to the stagnant pre-recorded tracks.

Hip-Hop is a style closely associated with rap music. It contains elements and characteristics normally attributed to rap-like repetitive drumbeats, bass lines, and melodies. It is often confused with rap music because many contemporary rappers use Hip-Hop tracks along with continuing to perform more traditional rap music. The differences are presently subtle, but in the future will become even more profound.

The main differences between rap and Hip-Hop are 1) the electronically produced drum sounds and samples not present in early rap music, 2) the interactive synthesizer and sampled arrangements not present in early rap music, 3) heavy swing and shuffle rhythms and grooves (i.e., New Jack Swing and Timbaland) not present in early rap music, 4) stripped-down rhythm and assorted variables within musical arrangements not present in early rap music. In other words, the main difference between rap and Hip-Hop is the development of distinct musical characteristics that were not borrowed (I'm being polite, actually stolen) from R&B. Although both styles employ rappers as a main focus, Hip-Hop uses unique form and structure along with vocal melodies and arrangements to accent the song.

Some music historians credit rap music's origins to the times of the post disco-era New York City urban music scene. This would mean that rap music came on the scene in the late 1970s as a result of young inner city kids using old R&B records as an underscore to their rap lyrics of desperation on the streets. This is only partially true. I definitely see the rap music phenomenon as East coast-based, but I argue that the exclusivity of New York City as rap's capital and any one group of inner city kids as the innovators is not entirely accurate. It is my view that music in America has developed on a continuum and the result is a cultural unity fully established within all types of African American forms of music. I argue that rap music, and by extension Hip-Hop, grew out of the universal principle of heavy rhythms, syncopation, African oral traditions, dance, and several other related influences that we will address in the content of this book.

Blues, funk, R&B, and jazz are all African American musical styles that drew from their African roots. They all contained rhythms, harmonies, melodies, and lyrics inspired from all walks of life, yet still shared the black experience in America. At the inception of all of these styles lies a struggle for acceptance from the white society. Hip-Hop is no exception.

The black musical experience has been one of many victories. In America as a whole, it has been one of victimization. It is commonly known that African Americans have had to bear the weight of the social and economic ills of this country. A result of this unbalanced weight can be seen as a mirror image in some respects of the greater society. In other words, in order to express oneself to an over-whelmingly adverse scrutiny, Hip-Hop had to reveal truths shared, yet unspoken, by all. The injustice leveled on young blacks could be blamed on the rap and Hip-Hop culture as a whole. Our society is ironically reflecting five basic ideals that are seen as a negative part of the rap and Hip-Hop world. They are 1) materialism: greed for wealth (money, cars, etc.), 2) sexual exploitation (glorification of pimps, hustlers, hookers, etc.), 3) over indulgence in drugs/alcohol (getting faded, busta 40s, gin & juice, etc.), 4) violence/gangs (gang banging, cop killa, smoking, wetting, etc.), and 5) vulgarity.

Even though many factions and cadres within the U.S. society are based around these exact same principles, the government and media at large target the rap and Hip-Hop world to shoulder the weight of these values. Socially speaking, rap music has gotten—forgive the pun—a bad rap. Some of the cons attributed to the rap and Hip-Hop community are exhibited by America as a whole.

Dead Presidents

Often American society has hypocritically criticized the rap community for its uncompromised position on the glory of material things. What is a rap lyric if it doesn't contain some allusion to money (ched-dar, broken off, Benjamins, dat paper, C notes, laced down, etc.) or cars for that matter? But with real-ity TV shows like "Fear Factor," "The Apprentice," endless prize shows, and the daily barrage of car commercials, there's no wonder why rappers are obsessed with the material. Money is an extreme motivating force in one's life when the alternative is, in many cases, prison or death on the streets.

Sex, Drugs, and Hip-Hop

Many people object to the images of tasteless bumping and grinding in many of the rap and Hip-Hop videos and concerts. The idea of promoting sexual images within a musical style is not a new one. Rock 'n' roll had its share of questionable sexual images. I've seen a few rock concerts that got a little out of hand. (Remember Woodstock? Or what about Live Aid?) In Hip-Hop it appears that neither male nor female is insulted over the loose moralistic ideas that they project. Women are debased and objectified as sex playthings. Men are often projected in packs or gangs with ungroomed baggy casual clothes. On the other hand, women are presented in herds with sexy and stylish tight-fitting clothes. Men are often thug-looking, with gold chains, tattoos, torn up grills, etc. Women are most often dolled up with perfect hair and nails and almost always looking their best. I consider this the "Ashanti/Jah Rule" concept!

Many rap and Hip-Hop images revolve around the idea of pimps and hustlers. Some Hip-Hoppers see that if you pimp someone you gain material things and/or sexual favors. If you hustle (the act of selling something that does not outright belong to you), you gain money to sustain your life without doing a "nine to five." Many people see having a hustle as being self-employed. An argument could be made that they had seen their parents get played, pimped, and hustled out of a decent life by the rich and powerful within this society. Many lyrics refer to these kind of exaggerated images of sexual roles and uneven relationships as normal in ethnic music.

I see this stereotype as a result of an accelerated or futuristic fantasy within the ethnic vision of sexuality. With so many song lyrics referring to possessing endless supplies of money, cars, jewelry, women, etc., there is a tendency to desire projecting or living out these fantasies in real life. In many ways this projection is being reinforced in our society with visual images of thug-styled life being more and more accepted. Motion pictures like *Get Rich or Die Trying* (starring 50 Cent) have stirred up controversy as to why filmmakers direct distorted messages of gang glory to the youth through films. Again, these stereotypical ideas have been borrowed from many other genres including blues and R&B.

Er'body in the Club Getting Tipsy

Drugs and alcohol have been a reality in the Hip-Hop world as it was in the R&B world, as it was in the rock world, and as it was in the blues world. What makes it different in today's society is what can only be seen as ignorance of the ill effects of drugs and alcohol on a person's life. Throughout the 1970s and '80s there have been several anti-drug and anti-alcohol movements nationwide urging young people to stay away from it. These movements were generally aimed at society at large and, in most cases, missed the ears and eyes of black youths. Many of these Hip-Hoppers grew up without both parents in the home. Most Hip-Hop era kids' parents were children during the "Super Fly" era when drugs and alcohol were shown in films as being a means to an end in a racist society. Black exploitation movies were very popular during the 1970s. The Goldie character from *The Mack* was a pimp. The Priest character from *Super Fly* was a drug dealer. Although these images were very powerful, they were only actors with no real power. The blame should not be laid at the feet of the motion picture industry entirely, but they were a huge influence. Drug addiction and alcoholism are an American epidemic. Drugs showed up in the ghetto, but they were not manufactured there. Now who really has power?

Who's the Real O.G.? "U.S. on Blast!"

Since the early days of the Roaring '20s, the United States has exhibited a culture of glorified violence. James Cagney and the Bowery Boys from the movies of the '30s and '40s, the Chicago gangland Eliot Ness movies and TV shows, and even biker gangs like the Hell's Angels of the 50s and '60s were all instrumental in shaping the minds of the youth. Gang violence even worked its way on to the Broadway musical stage, as in *West Side Story*. "O.G." means "original gangster." It would be fair to conclude that the original gangsters were Mafioso types operating in the existing corrupted American society. Illegal business deals, turf wars, executions, hit men, politicians, and cops on the take were all commonplace occurrences. Young people merely imitated what they saw on their streets.

Rap culture has been connected with stories of drive-by shootings, robberies, muggings, and other forms of terrorism. Much of this association is drawn by the news media. During the early 1980s, the local news media would bombard the TV with reports of gang shooting after gang shooting, and shrewdly depicted connections to these events to the black youth. This correlation resulted in a blanket indictment of rap music, and by extension, all black youth. Without any orientation of the history of these labels, the rap and Hip-Hop community embraced this image and like the "N word," turned being a gangster into being "gangsta'." Inasmuch, now this word has become a term of endearment. The result of the acceptance of these images by some of the Hip-Hop youth is outbreaks of violence, such as was exhibited when a brawl ensued during the Source Awards Show in 2000 and the Vibe Awards in 2004.

The Roof Is on Fire

As stated earlier, Hip-Hop has its own language, and in many ways it actually *is* its own language. The vernacular used in Hip-Hop is so coded it has become a way of expressing ideas and thoughts not fully represented in the dominant white culture. It is for this reason that throughout the course of this book I will refer to this type of speaking as *slanguage*.

In the past, the FCC has prohibited anyone from speaking obscenities or using vulgar words over the airwaves in the form of speech, poetry, or song. The same rules held true for television. Film, however, had more freedom of expression from almost its earliest inception. Censorship existed only in the form of ratings for films such as G, PG, R, X, and XXX. Generally speaking, all types of vulgar ideas—images and language—could be spoken of, depicted, and endorsed as long as the viewing audiences were pre-warned of its subject matter. Somewhere along the line, the language barrier line became blurred. Hip-Hop began warning its listeners of the language content and used four-letter words in lyrics, but so did the genres of rock, pop, R&B, blues, metal, and others. Street corner language has been around since street corners, so I hardly think that its use could be blamed on Hip-Hop. Just as a baby will pick up bad words from its parents, so does the Hip-Hop community pick up from its parents, the American society.

There are many Hip-Hop artists and songs that do not use bad language. Instead of calling congressional hearings to address these types of issues about the use of language on recordings, it may be more useful to mark the CDs more clearly and monitor its marketing, sale, and promotion a little more closely.

Hip-Hop music of today is a derivative of rap, R&B, pop, and rock music. In this book we will look at this influence and examine its musical components. I will show you how to interpret musical ideas with the feel and influence of the Hip-Hop music style in context to the period of time the music came on the scene.

Just as with R&B and pop music, certain instruments, textures, arrangements, and sounds became staples of those musical periods. We will explore these various uses and gain vital knowledge of how to reproduce these sounds both live and in the studio. The knowledge of reading notation will help you to study this book, but CD examples are also provided which show exactly how to play Hip-Hop music with authority.

Remember, without rap music there would be no Hip-Hop, so we must study the influence of rap music. The rapper is king in this style of music. The rhythm and the pulse of the rapper is the most important ingredient in the songs, so keyboard players should not play parts that are too busy and don't fit with the cadences and flow of the rap. Listen carefully to all rap and Hip-Hop songs so as to understand how the structures and forms developed over time.

Knowledge of Hip-Hop's characteristics can add to your ability to create keyboard parts that work well in existing Hip-Hop songs and even in songs you may want to compose. Also remember that Hip-Hop has crossed over to several other styles of music. For example, in smooth jazz, artists like Najee, Norman Brown, Gerald Albright, and many others routinely perform covers of Hip-Hop influenced songs such as Johnny Gill's "My, My, My," Janet Jackson's "That's the Way Love Goes," and TLC's "Waterfalls." Jazz artists such as the late Grover Washington, Jr., Miles Davis, and the Brecker Brothers experimented with Hip-Hop influenced recordings. Pop artists such as Britney Spears, Justin Timberlake, Lionel Richie, Michael Jackson, and many others dabble with Hip-Hop rhythms and concepts in their songs. Even country artists like Faith Hill, Dixie Chicks, and others blend Hip-Hop sounds and ideas into their song arrangements. Listen to the radio and see for yourself how many artists are now utilizing many of the ideas commonly associated with rap and Hip-Hop.

Be careful to establish the musical components that are unique to Hip-Hop so as not to mistake them for jazz, rock, and other styles. Even while you are using your creativity, you must subscribe to the existing rules of this style. All there is left to do now is read this book and learn about Hip-Hop. Are you ready?

Chapter One

1 EARLY RAP KEYBOARDS

In this chapter we will explore the patterns, rhythms and sounds that were established during the foundation of rap music. In an effort to fully understand these aspects, we will refer to some of the rap artists and their songs that were popular during this period of time. One of the earliest known rap songs was "Rapper's Delight," recorded by the Sugarhill Gang in 1982. Veteran R&B female vocalist Sylvia Robinson (known for her R&B hit single "Pillow Talk") discovered the Sugarhill Gang and was the group's producer. This song notably borrowed its entire music groove from a previously recorded song called "Good Times" by the R&B group called Chic. This combination of 1) an established rhythm groove or hit record, 2) a rapper (or DJ) speaking over it, and 3) an experienced record producer behind the scenes making decisions would be the success model for many more rap recordings for years to come. The rhythm used in that song and many others became a staple of the rap music genre.

Sugarhill Gang

Photo: Echos Archives, Redferns Music Picture Library

Like Dynamite Before It Blows! Boom!

As we all know, rappers don't sing. This is important for a number of reasons: 1) the urban youth did not have enough musical personalities and singers performing for them that they could relate to; 2) in 1979, music instruction in the schools was being phased out, specifically in urban schools making it nearly impossible to obtain or learn an instrument; 3) many talented songwriters and musicians historically were not known as singers nor did they always possess the skill of singing, therefore rappers did not feel the need to have to sing at all; 4) if you had a gift for rhyming and making beats (including "beat boxing"), you could become a celebrity yourself; and lastly, 5) if you owned a turntable, you didn't really need to hire a band or approach one to play for you for that matter because you could simply play the record. Some of the most popular rap artists of the early days were Kurtis Blow, Grandmaster Flash, Melle Mel, Kool Moe Dee, MC Lyte, J.J. Fad, Heavy D, Doug E. Fresh, LL Cool J, Run-DMC, Donald D, the Fat Boys, and a myriad of others.

Where Did Rap Come From?

The earliest rap recording I can remember was called "Here Comes the Judge" by David Pigmeat Markham. This song came out sometime during the early 1960s. Even though this was considered an R&B song, all one had to do is listen to the introduction of drums and rap vocals to fully understand that rap music has been around for much longer than we thought. Pigmeat started his career in the 1920s as a vaudeville act. The influence of music, dance, and theatre influenced his early rhapsodizing or "slang" rap. It was the performance of rapid-fire comedy in minstrel music theatre that gave Pigmeat an outlet to explore his efforts of rap. During the 1940s, Pigmeat, Bessie Smith, and especially Louis Jordan, led the way in introducing this minstrel influence on early recordings. Each of these artists used jump blues rhythms, clever lyrics, and rhapsodizing monologues both live and in the studio. It's no wonder that James Brown credits Louis Jordan as being his single strongest musical influence. Needless to say, James Brown—the undisputed Godfather of Soul and creator of funk music—has been a huge influence on early rap and Hip-Hop to this very day. In jazz music,

James Moody's "Moody's Mood for Love" can easily be seen as vocal rhapsodizing. Equally jazz-inspired is Webster Lewis's "Kemo-Kimo," a tongue twister, but clever rhythmic rap lyric. Even early blues songs like "I'll Put a Spell on You" by Screamin' Jay Hawkins had rap-inspired lyrics. So, at closer look, the correlation is a close one and demonstrates cultural unity within African American music, which has a strong foundation in vocal rhythms and poetry. In fact, African traditional music included vocal improvisation and drum beat from the very inception of music itself.

The word *rhapsodize* means: 1) to express oneself in an immoderately enthusiastic manner, and 2) to recite something in the manner of a rhapsody. If this is so, then poetry, spoken word, and church sermons could be considered rap. In the early to late 1960s, poetry and rhapsodizing were gaining popularity from the beatnik movement and the "Last Poets" style rap inspired by the Black Panther movement. The raw street language, in-your-face subject matter, and racial awareness made music's role in protesting the war, unfair social conditions, and economic inequities a little more inspiring.

R&B and Its Relationship with Early Rap

In order to fully understand rap music, you must look into its origins in R&B music of the 1960s and 1970s. For example, the Jimmy Castor Bunch recorded a song called "Troglodyte" that included an extended rhythm beat and rap intro. This was done for the purpose of effect and to secure a solid dance beat for the young listener. The song is an R&B classic and was a huge hit. James Brown referred to rap in almost all of his lyrics (i.e., "Funky President"). Rap's influence can be heard in the rated X comedy of the 1960s recording artist Rudy Ray Moore and his Dolemite fame. The Stax Records artists Carla Thomas (daughter of Rufus Thomas) and the legendary Otis Redding scored a big hit with the funky and scandalous song "Tramp." This song was one of many to come that started out with the break beat rhythm as an intro along with the rap duet right off the bat. This proved to be a winning formula for rap arrangements.

Doo-Wop, Soul, and Their Relationship with Early Rap

One could argue that the Moonglows' "Ten Commandments of Love" is rap-inspired. Many of the doo-wop groups of the 1950s through to the 1970s used rap monologues in their song arrangements as well as in live performance. Soul music artists also played a huge role in the use of rhapsodizing. Brook Benton's "The Boll Weevil Song" and Clarence Carter's "Patches" both utilized clever rap banter and vocal rhythms that would influence rap. Marlena Shaw's "Go Away Little Boy," James Brown's "King Heroin," Barry White's ballads, Shirley Brown's "Woman to Woman," Barbara Mason's "Shacking Up," and many of the rated X songs of Millie Jackson were known to include rap monologues.

Funk and Its Relationship with Early Rap

Funk artists and songs like the Ohio Players' "Funky Worm," Parliament's "Chocolate City," and Lakeside's "Fantastic Voyage" were all forerunners of the early days of rap and Hip-Hop music. It was first the funk artists who were bold enough to deal with relevant issues in their lyrics. Gil Scott-Heron's "The Revolution Will Not Be Televised" and "B Movie" were angry political protest raps. Funkadelic songs routinely contained raps and monologues that were clearly preludes to rap music. Charles Wright & the Watts 103rd St. Band brought "Express Yourself" into the funk scene utilizing the "preach style" rap vocals. Funk artists always used the powerful and syncopated rhythms that made the young people want to dance. Rap music has a profoundly identifiable funk root within its sound and style.

From Pop & Lock to Hip 'n' Hop

Dance music has always inspired the youth in America. From the early 1920s Jitterbug to Hip-Hop dance, music has been created to fit within the culture and influence of dance. Rock 'n' roll sock hops often were hyped by the local DJs using their slang with the music to get the kids dancing. Country square-dance events would also use the auctioneer-style rapping with the music to get the country kids up to the beat and dancing. It was during these early days of the 1950s and 1960s that the DJ became an important part of the musical formula and was soon to be seen as inseparable from the style itself.

Pigmeat Markham's "Here Comes the Judge" became so popular during the mid 1960s that the song hook was made a permanent skit on the popular TV show "Rowan & Martin's Laugh-In." This skit included famous singer/actor Sammy Davis, Jr. Notably, the song was remade by Shorty Long in 1968. Its tempo was made faster and funkier so as to fit with the dance crazes. Dance styles like the "Twist," the "Mashed Potatoes," the "Watusi," the "Monkey," and the "Swim" were all accompanied by hit songs from a variety of artists.

None of these songs, however, could be considered dance styles—they were merely funky dances. The earliest song name that I can recall that named a dance style was "The Breakdown" by Rufus Thomas. The songs of James Brown included hits and breaks. These hits and breaks were inspired by Brown's earliest influence of jump blues stops and accents. Rufus Thomas followed in Brown's footsteps with these types of effects in "Walking the Dog," "Push and Pull," "Funky Chicken," and "The Breakdown." During this time, early rap songs like "Barefootin'" by Robert Parker, "The Name Game" by Shirley Ellis, and "One Eye Open" by The Maskman and the Agents were very popular with young dancers. The rhapsodizing approach was catching on internationally with dance-influenced efforts like "Soul Makossa" by Manu Dibango which featured funky music and a rap. Instrumentals like Dennis Coffey and the Detroit Guitar Band's "Scorpio" and Billy Preston's "Outa-Space" were hot dance floor sides. If you listen closely, you will hear elements of Hip-Hop.

During the early 1970s, a popular show called "Soul Train" made its debut. Host Don Cornelius gave the young dancers an opportunity to premier all the latest dances so that new dances would be seen nationally and new dance crazes would get started. The bright colored fashions, hair styles, and accessories would influence the way the music would be experienced. On one of the tapings of "Soul Train," a young talented girl who appeared as a regular on the show did an impromptu solo dance with guest R&B artist, Joe Tex. Joe Tex, like James Brown and Rufus Thomas, was well-known for his preach style rap singing. This was proven perfect for the *break beat* scene. Joe Tex performed his hit called "I Got Ya" with this young woman as the object of his interest. This young woman's name was DaMita Jo Freeman. She, along with most of the young people on the show, was responsible for the dance style known as *Pop & Lock*.

Shake It Like a Bowl of Soup, Make It Go Loopty Loop

A group of young dancers emerged on the scene in the early 1970s consisting of colorful young teens nicknamed Boogaloo Sam, Flukey Luke, and Shabba Doo (who choreographed and appeared in the *Breakin'* movies). Along with the group's leader, Don Campbell, they changed the landscape of dance forever! This group was called the Lockers. They appeared on several TV shows and novelty specials and always got a fantastic response. Even Fred "Re-Run" Berry (of the TV show "What's Happening!!") did a stint with the Lockers. These very popular dancers put the spotlight on Pop & Lock and opened the door for the evolution of Hip-Hop. This type of dance style combined numerous interpretations of existing dances with a free-style or improvised approach. Known dances like the "Breakdown," the "4-Corners," and the "Robot" were now being performed with costumes, skits, and props just as Pigmeat Markham had done twenty years earlier in his vaudeville routines.

In fact, during this period Pigmeat Markham scored another hit with his song and dance craze known as "Truckin'." Soul artist and former Temptation Eddie Kendricks would later make a hit with his dance-inspired song called "Keep On Truckin'." This song used many swing rhythms that are now stylized in Hip-Hop.

Since the concept of the *break* (rhythmic and percussion patterns included as accents for dancers) was added to R&B and funk arrangements, the DJ and dancers had a spot in the song where they could do their thing. For at least a few bars, the DJ could rap over the music and the dancers could get busy. This kind of pattern became known as *break beats*. James Brown's original drummer, Clayton Fillyau is believed to have invented the first break beat from an improvised solo during a 1962 *Live at the Apollo* recording. Ever since then, his beat has been sampled as a principal break beat!

By the end of the 1970s, pop & lock dancing was becoming passé. Young people were searching for a more dynamic expression of dance. With the adage "everything old is new again," they looked back to the 1940s Nicholas Brothers form of acrobatic hoofing and dancing. These activities included head spinning, wall running, back twisting, tumbling crazy legs, splits, and other gymnastic-type moves.

The Afro-Brazilian dance/martial art form of Capoera has been credited as the original early form of break dancing. Many of these movements are borrowed from traditional Angolan African movement as well. They named this type of dancing from the break beat rhythms that inspired it. Pop & Lock dance eventually evolved into break dancing and became the definitive dance of rap and, by extension, Hip-Hop. If you look closely at the break dancers' moves, they clearly start their break dance moves with a "rubber legs" step from the "Charleston" which is considered a derivative of the "Jitterbug."

Go-Go Music and Break Beats

In the early 1970s, a Jamaican born (Bronx transplant) New York DJ named Clive Campbell, also known as Kool DJ Herc, was getting acclaim for being an innovator of break beat radio mixing. In other words, Herc would layer record after record back to back with the rhythm breaks on the recordings taking center stage. This was very clever but he was not the first or the last to do it. In fact, every major city had its own local DJ celebrities. In St. Louis we had Dr. Jockenstein, Al Kool Gator, and Curtis Soul. All of these personalities were known for spinning records at parties, mixing DJ fades on the air, and acting as master of ceremonies (Emcee) for concert events. Hence, the idea of "MC So-and-So" became the norm.

In addition to break beats, go-go style rhythms and grooves were gaining popularity in the Washington, D.C. area. A lot of the clubs would feature female dancers on platforms or via poles to highlight the break rhythms and grooves similar to the 1960s style go-go dancers from psychedelic pop. D.C.-based go-go was more funk rooted and was swing heavy. Chuck Brown and the Soul Searchers' recording of "Bustin' Loose" and, similarly later, "Da Butt" by E.U. inspired the rhythms that would ignite the 1990s "New Jack Swing" style.

Nine Rap Forms

Rap music can essentially be put into nine basic forms. This by no means limits the types of forms there will ever be, but rather puts into some perspective the presently existing types. All of these forms include the music and the rhythm as its additional ingredient.

1. **Poetic Rap**   Using rhythmless poetry to accent the music (Me'Shell Ndegeocello or Floetry)

2. **Spoken Word**   Using words disconnected to express whole ideas (Jill Scott/Mos Def or Gil Scott-Heron)

3. **Rhythm Rap**   Using vocal rhythm to rap to the beat, common rap (Heavy D, Eminem, Tupac, 50 Cent)

4. **Slam Rap**   Using the act of dissing competitively live on stage (National Poetry Slams, the Dozens, Dolemite)

5. **Preach Rap**   Using preacher monotone melodic rhythms in rap (Nelly, Busta Rhymes, Speech with Arrested Development)

6. **Free Style**   Using slanguage to improvise rap ideas on the spot (street corner, radio, call-in, amateur rappers)

7. **Gangsta Rap**   Using ghetto slang, violent lyrics, and vulgarity (Ghetto Boyz, N.W.A., Snoop Dogg)

8. **Monologue**   Using Ole School narration to musical sections (Mary J. Blige, Missy Elliott, Common)

9. **Spittin'**   Using anger as a motive to rap about problems (Public Enemy, Furious Five, Lil' Jon, Run-DMC, DMX, Pitbull, Ice Cube)

No Disrespect

A deep-rooted tradition in African culture is the idea of **Esu Elegbara**. This is a Yoruba term that refers to an ancient mythology describing a personality or deity that uses tongue-twisting stories in order to humiliate or confuse people it encounters. This deity speaks in riddles and creates verbal dilemmas in order to control the mind. In other words, the Esu Elegbara is the spirit of verbal sparring in order to gain victory over an oral opponent. In many of these ancient cultures, the deity is depicted as a monkey. Out of this idea came the African American concept of the Signifying Monkey. Obviously, this idea deserves much research and study; however, the art or the act of signifying has become a common African American oral tradition. The black youth in America have always participated in competitive word games, whether it be on the playgrounds, schoolyards, or on rap stages.

As a result of this type of commonplace verbal game, many other forms of insult for entertainment emerged. From the 1920s to the present, blacks teens have engaged in street games like spinning tops, marbles, mumbly peg, stickball, and of course, craps. The art of rapping phrases while rolling the dice ("Mama needs a new pair of shoes," etc.) eventually became known as "playing the dozens." The "dozens" refers to the largest roll of two dice, which was twelve. In the billiard halls, on the streets, or wherever the hangouts were, there was always someone talking about the other's mother or insulting them directly. Even though this custom of talking about one's mother was seen among friends as a kind of friendly fun, it could get serious and physical if the insults continued too much.

Over time this idea of talking about someone—ragging, snaps, bagging, signifying, Jones'n, or playing the dozens—extended itself to making unwarranted threats of violence. Although the threats were often idle, one could get into trouble for "selling too many woof tickets." No one really knows why this way of accelerating an argument has been dubbed "woof tickets," but it must have something to do with being dogged. Maybe it came from the "bark is bigger than the bite" adage. At any rate, the dozens, woofing, and dissing are here to stay.

Throughout the history of blues, rock 'n' roll, R&B, and jazz, artists have had competitive conflicts and personal animosity towards other artists in their genre. Since these artists competed for the same market and performed many of the same types of songs and shows, there were jealousies and acts of sabotage on the road and in the studios. For the most part, these acts and attitudes were kept well hidden from the public. It was considered unprofessional to belittle a fellow artist onstage or on recordings. In fact, it was the norm to actually appear congenial in public to an artist who in private life may even be a mortal enemy. This was the way rival acts demonstrated mutual respect.

During the early 1970s, the group Funkadelic broke this mold by recording the very first "DIS" (disrespect) record. The song that made fun of artists like Rufus; Kool & the Gang; and Earth, Wind & Fire was called "Let's Take It to the Stage." Although this song was composed as a parody and was done in good fun, it did raise a few eyebrows and burned a couple of bridges.

Following in the footsteps of this trend were rap artists like Notorious B.I.G. vs. Tupac, Eazy-E vs. N.W.A., East Coast vs. West Coast, and Nas vs. Jay-Z. Rap artists' feuds and dissing continues throughout today's world of Hip-Hop.

Chant Vocals and Audience Response

Throughout the R&B era, artists would employ audience participation techniques to hype the live experience. They would use tried and true vocal rhythms to get everybody involved. One of the innovators of chant vocals was the great Cab Calloway with his world-renowned chant, "HI DI HI DI HI DI HO!" Throughout the decades some of these vocal "hollas" (hollers) were "call and responses" such as "Hey…ho…paar-tay, dum di dum di-i-yi," the Londonary-influenced "Get on down and par-tay," "Get off!" and Prince's patented "Oowa oowa."

At the crossroads of R&B and rap, the vocal hollas became more aggressive and more vulgar. It seemed that the audiences would not respond as well unless they were allowed to chant some of these mantra-like phrases. Some of these chants were "Shit goddam, get off your ass and jam," "The roof is on fire," and "We don't need no water, let the mutha fucka burn." As I'm sure you could guess, this served to open the door to the acceptance of rough language in rap lyrics. Things have gotten off the heezee for sheezee my neezee! Nowadays, Hip-Hop phrases include chants like the popular "Hip-Hop Hurray" recorded by Naughty By Nature, "Hey…ho," "Woomp there it is," "Who let the dogs out?", "Somebody scream," and "Roof, roof" (dog barkings).

Cut Creator

Rap music and Hip-Hop as a whole have been transformed by the creative musicality of the *Mix Masters.* The DJs (or Spinners, Scratchers or Turn-table artists) like the late great Jam Master Jay from Run-DMC or Def Jam's Kid Capri helped to define the music. This will be covered in depth in Chapter 9. However, it is notable to mention now that we cannot understate the need to understand the role of the DJ in Hip-Hop.

The "Ole School" versions of the Cut Creators were the **Remix Producers**. Back in the early 1970s, a movement emerged for music producers to splice several hit songs into a single song that could be used as a parody skit. This musical skit would include voice-overs, narration, and comedic punch lines to segue from one hook to the next. These types of recordings were usually low budget productions that didn't always adhere to copyright laws of usage but always got a good laugh. One such recording was called "Superfly Meets Shaft." This remix was written by John & Ernest and was produced by Dickie Goodman. Even though this song was not taken seriously by the recording industry, in my opinion it could now be seen as the advent of the remix and the inception of the sampled rap hook. If so, then this discovery was a profound one indeed!

Parody and Novelty Rap

During the early days of rap another phenomenon occurred. Many comedians and novelty acts began cutting rap records in order to gain more exposure and capitalize on a rising craze. It was believed by many at that time that rap would only be a fad. Since fads were thought of as short-lived, an entertainer could take the money and run.

Even though pioneers like Rudy Ray Moore had been doing rap-like recordings for years, he was thought of as a rated X performer who would never make it to the radio airwaves. Older 1960s records like "Monster Mash" by Bobby Boris Pickett and others like it were pseudo-cult classics of a sort, but not to be taken seriously. In the early 1970s, comedian Bill Cosby recorded a hilarious tune called "Hicky Burr." This song was produced by Quincy Jones and was notorious for its break sections featuring Cosby's James Brown-like vocal Brown-isms. I actually loved that song. It wasn't until the early 1980s that parody made another big resurgence.

In 1981, Frankie Smith recorded "Double Dutch Bus" which was a rap song that became a huge hit. It was on the radio night and day and was sure to keep the dance floor filled with its infant-like rap-isms. In 1985, Rappin' Duke, who was produced by veteran H.B. Barnum, made quite a political splash that stirred up controversy because of his unabashed rip-off of legendary actor John Wayne. The name of Duke's song was simply titled "Da Ha." Notably, rapper Too Short would later rerecord a hit of his own called "Blow-Job Betty" with music taken from Rappin' Duke. Other parodies would follow, like comedian Rodney Dangerfield's "Rappin' Rodney," Eddie Murphy's "Honeymooner's Rap," Blondie (featuring Deborah Harry) with "Rapture," and even a California Raisins' rap. The Fat Boys' "All You Can Eat," DJ Jazzy Jeff & the Fresh Prince's "Parents Just Don't Understand," Biz Markie's "U Got What I Need" and "Vapors," Eminem's "Slim Shady," and Sir Mix-A-Lot's "Baby Got Back" were all successful novelty rap songs.

Rap Keyboard Players

Rap keyboard players were usually young and did not know much about musical notation or theory. There were also those who were skilled in other styles and simply added rap to their repertoire. Many players did, however, have an excellent knowledge of rhythm, feel, and groove, which was of the utmost importance: rap music is all about rhythm.

The knowledgeable rap keyboard players of that day had played R&B and funk. They were aware of all of the rhythmic placements and variations that their parts needed to have. Rap keyboard players needed this skill in order to support the rappers within the song structure. Those who were not really musicians but played a little keyboard also were listening to the music of the day and were equally aware of how the music should be played within the rhythmic structure that was foundation in those styles. Untrained rap keyboard players had an equally profound effect on rap music just as the ones who were well-trained did. Their drum programming abilities and their sparse keyboard parts significantly demonstrated the lasting effect they had. The parts they created were usually sampled or they actually played chords and rhythms. The result was keyboard parts that were used merely as effect rather than melodically or harmonically. Some look at this as being non-musical, however, I see it as unique and ingenious.

Since live music was fading fast and many rappers were in search of recreations of recorded hit tracks, the rap keyboard player became highly in demand for recording sessions as a musician and as a producer. The thing that made rap keyboard players unique was the new ways they were using these instruments and the bold ways they were changing arrangements, song form, and the tonality (ambience) of urban music. One particular song called "The Message" typified this change of ambience and expanded sense of rap rhythm. This song was recorded by Grandmaster Flash & the Furious Five.

"The Message" contains parts, rhythms, and effects that are almost exclusively keyboard. Some of the early rap keyboard players like Tyrone Brunson, Kashif, Randy Muller, Hubert Eaves, David Frank, Bernard Wright, Dexter Wansel, and many others helped to solidify this genre. Their use of rhythm sounds and effects helped to establish rap as we know it. They knew that live keyboard sounds and arrangements were becoming old fashioned and outdated.

They were looking for a new sound and new way of playing without sounding so sophisticated. They were keyboard players, not just piano players who played a synthesizer. Generally speaking, rap keyboard players were embracing the studio quality and stripped-down sound that the public was becoming fond of.

Rap music had a heavy repetitive feel and pulse to it. It was designed to make you dance. It was a direct result and natural evolution of the disco era moving mainstream. The younger generation that grew up in the early 1980s were, as young children, exposed to disco and pseudo-R&B of the late 1970s. The early rap generation cut their teeth on disco dance music. Disco was also repetitive dance music but it was directed to the older crowd who frequented nightclubs and discotheques and was quickly becoming passé. R&B was becoming so heavily produced that it did not appeal to the younger inner-city blacks that were rapidly feeling lost and left out of the musical scene.

Rap keyboard players also had a pretty good understanding of the technical aspects of their chosen instrument. For example, if they needed to add more attack to a synth sound, they knew how to edit and modify existing on-board presets. Some of them had synthesizer programming skills. They had to learn to operate the latest keyboard equipment before anyone else did or they would find themselves behind the times and unemployed. This lack of equipment knowledge was and still is unacceptable for a cutting edge rap keyboard player.

Since the rap keyboard player is generally independent, they usually understand the recording studio environment very well. They are equally skilled in sequencing techniques. In the Hip-Hop world this is simply called "making beats" or "bustin' tracks." This art of arranging for Hip-Hop is a desired skill and is probably why you are interested in this book.

As discussed in the introduction, rap music has been around for several decades and is still prevalent in much of the contemporary black music genre. Contemporary R&B and Hip-Hop contain elements of rap music, and its influence can be heard in styles ranging from smooth jazz to urban rock and pop. The keyboard plays an integral role in the overall sound of rap music. In the early years of rap (1979–1985), most musical arrangements contained synthesized keyboard sounds, bass sounds, and drum sounds. The keyboard, in many cases, was the instrument which generated most of the sounds used on actual rap recordings.

Manufacturers such as Roland, Oberheim, Yamaha, and Korg produced polyphonic synthesizers that could be used as the sonic sketch pad for rap music's harmonic colors. Even though the Moog synthesizer was still being used to produce synthesized bass lines and lead-line melodies, other sounds were beginning to be used in the place of guitar and piano sounds. The sounds used were polyphonic synthesizer brass sounds, bells, pads, and thin lead sounds. Sampled sounds and sound effects were often layered within the rhythm tracks. We will discuss these samples and other ambience in a later chapter of this book.

Early Rap Playing Examples

The following examples are presented in order to familiarize students with the sounds, rhythms, and techniques commonly associated with rap keyboard parts. They contain parts commonly found in early rap recordings. Notice how the sounds used for each part are those used in 1970s R&B music. Sounds like acoustic piano, strings, Rhodes, polyphonic synthesized brass, and lead synthesizers were often featured in early rap songs. Each exercise is first presented with rhythm accompaniment and keyboards. Then, after a brief pause, the tune is played again without the keyboard parts so you can play along. Students may follow the notation provided or pick out the parts by ear.

Delightful Rap

TRACK 1

Messages

TRACK 2

Married Fast

TRACK 3

Nasty

Funky Heartbeat

TRACK 6

Chapter Two

2 EARLY HIP-HOP KEYBOARDS

In the early days of Hip-Hop, keyboard parts centered around the groove of the recording. Most recordings of this music were either sampled or they imitated the feel and hooks of existing hit songs. The disco era was just about nearing a close, but the desire for rhythmic and danceable grooves remained strong. As stated earlier, R&B music had been the forerunner of heavy groove music, but the arrangements were becoming a little too sophisticated for the younger audience. The kids in the inner city were searching for a new style that would give them the funky repetitive drum and bass back-beat they were used to, but still offer them a fresher approach to the song form. Rap had already taken them there with the lyrical content and break-beat hyped sections. The only ingredients missing were the structure, form, and sound to give Hip-Hop its uniqueness.

Traditionally, keyboard parts in other dance styles were played melodically with heavy emphasis on the harmony in the song. Blues, funk, R&B, and soul all used keyboards as orchestration. The guitar and the vocals carried the main thrust of these genres. Hip-Hop broke that mold by using keyboard parts that accented the drums, the rap lyrics, and especially the bass lines. In 1981, Taana Gardner recorded the song "Heartbeat," a funky and hip-hopping groove that laid the foundation for many Hip-Hop songs to come. The popular female vocal group, Seduction, later recorded this song. The movement toward this type of arrangement had begun in the early 1980s, but didn't totally gel until around 1985, when Hip-Hop really became defined. Some of the earliest Hip-Hop artists were Afrika Bambaataa & Zulu Nation, Grandmaster Flash & the Furious Five, Kurtis Blow, Ice-T, Run-DMC, KRS-One & BDP, Ultramagnetic MCs, and a few others.

Techno Funk and the Synthesizer

During the mid 1980s, artists and songs like Tyrone Brunson's "The Smurph," D-Train's "You're the One for Me," Marvin Gaye's "Gotta Give It Up," Brick's "Dazz," The System's "You Are in My System," and many other keyboard-heavy songs began to set the stage for more simplified but aggressive songs. The use of techno sounds and polyphonic synthesizers, powerful monophonic synthesized bass parts, and sweeping analog synth effects were becoming more and more commonplace in early Hip-Hop arrangements.

Techno pop keyboard sounds began to cross lines and end up on Hip-Hop records. Afrika Bambaataa was one of the pioneers of techno influenced Hip-Hop. He used synthesizers for chords and leads. Bambaataa and his group Zulu Nation was created in 1979 and was one of the first rap groups. Bambaataa also created Soul Sonic Force and is now a Hip-Hop icon! His hit song "Planet Rock" was filled with distinct techno synthesizer parts. Techno & Hip-Hop grooves were almost always funky, with heavy processed drums accented by powerful piano and bass sounds. The influence of early Hip-Hop arrangements was evident in the songs and arrangements of artists such as Lisa Lisa & Cult Jam, Full Force, C+C Music Factory, Ready for the World, and many other acts. As stated earlier, rap producers were instrumental in defining the way a keyboard player would approach arranging their parts. One of the reasons for this is that the producer was often the musician who

Afrika Bambaataa

would develop tracks in the studio or arrange preproduction tracks at home in his/her personal studio. Producers like Hubert Eaves III, Jimmy Jam & Terry Lewis, Teddy Riley, David Frank, Kashif, and many others contributed to the formation and origins of early Hip-Hop keyboards.

The Influence of the Drum Machine

The drum machine was a device used to produce and record rhythms/beats within the electronic realm of MIDI. Its ability to sync up to computers, keyboards, and other recording gear made it an ideal tool for MIDI recording. In the early stages of Hip-Hop, the sampling laws were being challenged and redefined. Taking an existing hit record and rapping over it was easier. Not being able to do so after the laws changed in the mid 1980s, made it difficult to create funky grooves that had the rhythms that locked in the musical hooks. The uses of previously released recordings had become illegal. Record companies, songwriters, and producers were beginning to challenge the authority of Hip-Hop artists to use their songs

Drum machine from the early '80s

without permission and rerecording deals. Songwriters and live musicians were demanding a greater share in the recording process. The drum machine became a great friend of the Hip-Hop world for quite a few reasons.

Using the drum machine became a way for Hip-Hop producers to create new grooves with the tried and true funky feel of the old-school beats. The rhythm was steady, heavy, and even almost as powerful as some of the old James Brown grooves. If a producer could recreate a drum groove of an old hit record on his machine, add some new synthesized sounds to it, and beef up the arrangement, the show could go on.

For some unknown reason, live drummers had great difficulty emulating the rhythms, patterns, and feel that Hip-Hop producers were creating. Only a handful of live drummers were able to effectively play some of these creative beats. So this meant that the demand for a strong Hip-Hop drummer became great. Unlike the keyboard players, drummers did not embrace a lot of new drum technological designs and sounds. They didn't bother learning about the machines' operation and potential. This served to open the door for the producers to define the drum rhythms from their inception. Most of the time the Hip-Hop producer was either a keyboardist himself/herself, or composed from his/her keyboard. It is also notable that during this period of time, guitar parts became sparse and in many cases non-existent on Hip-Hop records as well. This was the case because most Hip-Hop producers only knew keyboards and either couldn't or wouldn't hire guitar players. Another reason for the omission of the live drum and guitar parts on early Hip-Hop records is that the Hip-Hop artist wouldn't be able to recreate their parts live. Additionally, guitar parts had to be performed live and couldn't be MIDI recorded. Since digital recorders didn't exist yet, this meant one would have to record a guitar player old-school style with expensive analog recorders and sound studios. A drum machine and keyboard parts *could* be performed live via MIDI.

During the early to mid 1980s, the studios were starting to make the transition from analog to digital recording technology. Along with this transition came the problem of recording a song with a small budget. All of the traditional analog studios were very expensive and required a lot of real-time recording techniques that included many overdubs and passes. Since Hip-Hop was experimental at that time, it became more cost effective to record as much as possible via MIDI.

In most cases, a MIDI arrangement was all that was necessary to track a Hip-Hop record. With an experienced producer, engineer, and great outboard effects, it was then possible to produce a record without a live drummer. As unbelievable as it sounded, it really was possible.

With the impossible made probable, many Hip-Hop records hit the shelves with programmed grooves and experimental sounds, and Hip-Hop was born. No longer was an old-school R&B hit needed to sample a funky groove. Keyboards and drum machines were the magical instruments that made the one-man band idea a reality. We will revisit this drum machine topic in detail in Chapter 6 in the section called "Making a Hip-Hop Track."

The following examples demonstrate the way early Hip-Hop keyboard parts were performed in songs. Pay careful attention to the placement of the rhythms and the sounds used. Piano was a sound that, for the most part, Hip-Hop was trying to phase out. Remember that the style at this point in time was being defined. Artists and producers were attempting to solidify the overall Hip-Hop feel, groove and sound. A funky beat, heavy accents, contemporary sounds, and repetitive patterns were the desired effect. Don't forget to include the street attitude that can be felt on each recording of this era.

In "Hip Planet," notice how the drum machine is accenting more syncopated rhythms. The bass part is moving with the kick drum while the string part plays an eerie melody. The melody is based on the Phrygian mode, a mode still used in modern Hip-Hop lines of today. This groove is not unlike grooves by Afrika Bambaataa of the 1980s.

Hip Planet

TRACK 7

"School Time" consists of some nice chords played on the Rhodes to accent the funky Hip-Hop beat laid down by the bass and drums. Listen for the syncopation between the horn part and the scratch rhythm.

School Time

TRACK 8

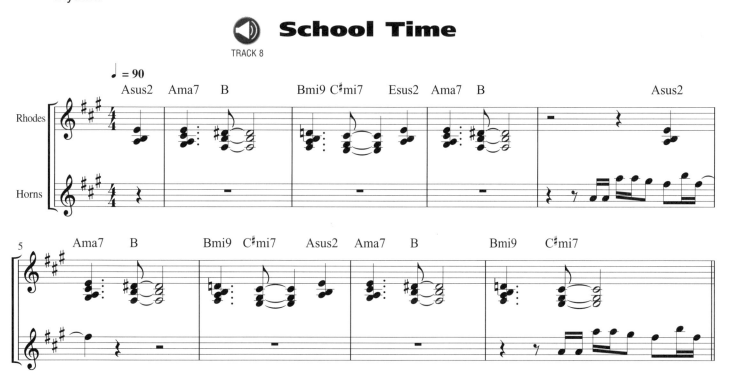

In "Hype Type," the string sound lights the fuse for the hits to bounce chromatically up and down throughout this nice groove. Notice the vocal snippets and drone synthesizer line.

Hype Type

TRACK 9

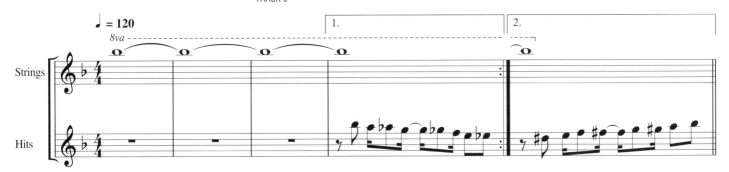

In "Jazzy Taste," the Rhodes part has a swing feel to it as the lead line glides through the funky sophisticated groove. Be careful transitioning into the abrupt ending.

Jazzy Taste

TRACK 10

The bell pad and the electric piano in "Jah Love" need to sound together. Take your time and try to feel all of the subtle rhythms provided by the drum machine part.

Jah Love

TRACK 11

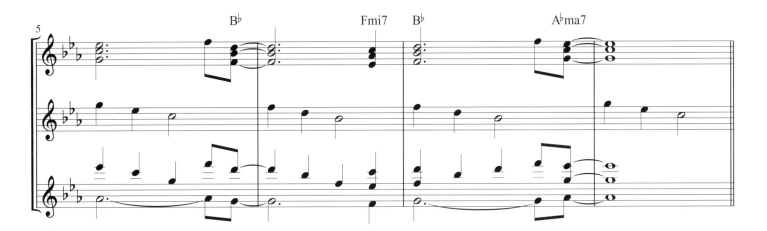

"Lyte Groove" uses a Kalimba sound which takes the lead. As simple and as straight as this part is, it might be challenging to play perfectly in time. Practice slowly, then nail it.

Lyte Groove

In "Wolf Ticket," the synthesizer line is played unison with the bass line. This was common in the early days of Hip-Hop keyboards. See if you can tell why this one is titled "Wolf Ticket."

Wolf Ticket

"Hip-Hop Cheer" features the lead line synthesizer playing a glide or **portamento** between octaves. Your synthesizer should have this effect on board. If not, use a left-hand glissando to imply this effect. Good luck.

Hip-Hop Cheer

TRACK 14

Chapter Three

3

THE RHYTHM OF MAKING BEATS

The keys to playing effective Hip-Hop grooves are understanding rhythms, establishing a solid foundation rooted in the drums, and engaging in the activity of creating or improvising beats. These three key elements are at the root of any musician, singer or rapper expressing themselves within the genre of Hip-Hop. As simple as this concept may seem, it requires a great deal of preparation in terms of listening to style and character, developing the ear, and of course, improvising patterns that make sense without making mistakes and sounding weak.

The first thing you need to do is start using your body to physically internalize or absorb the rhythms. It is a good idea to get used to tapping your feet, clapping your hands, or even thumping the chest or lap in the old "ham bone" fashion in order to keep good time and become comfortable with rhythms.

Another good idea is to start right now trying to **beat box**. This is the technique that is applied when using your mouth and voice in such a way as to imitate the sounds and patterns of a drum kit being played by a great drummer. In 1988, Hip-Hop artist Doug E. Fresh recorded *Children's Story* which featured a great beat box song called "La Di Da Di." This was one of the first *a cappella* Hip-Hop tunes, and it featured beat box master, Slick Rick. Even the Fat Boys broke new musical ground with their unique brand of vocal beat box. Beat boxing may seem a little odd and may even be awkward to do at first, but it is one of the most effective ways for someone to become introduced to the world of making beats. It is a good idea to start off with drumbeats you already know pretty well and have no problem remembering. Use one of your favorite Hip-Hop songs. When you get over the shock of making funny sounds with your mouth, you'll begin to find it fun and rewarding.

Boom Shacka Lacka Lacka Boom Shacka Lack Boom Da

Present throughout the history of African American music is the practice of vocal rhythm and early beat-box concepts. In blues, Muddy Waters showed us "How How How How," and when we learned we "Boom Boom Boom Boomed." In R&B, vocal rhythms like "Shoo Be Doo Be Doo Be Doo Da Day" and "La La La La La La La La La" have always been used in rhythmic patterns that were fun and easy for people to sing. Sly Stone used many vocal beat-box ideas and tongue twisters like "Shadrack, Meshack & Abednego" as clever rhythmic accents. Originating in jazz, **scatting** became so common that to this very day it is used in many other styles and taught as an approach to improvising. Louis Armstrong, Ella Fitzgerald, and Cab Calloway (Hi Dee Hi Dee Hi Dee Ho), as well as many others, specialized in scat rhythms. In Hip-Hop, Heavy D is one of the most rhythmic rappers ever. His rap group Heavy D & the Boyz have a song called "My Diddley Diddley Diddely Dee," which is one of the toughest raps to rap. The examples within all genres are abundant.

Heavy D & the Boyz

Another idea is to dance. Not everyone is blessed with great dancing ability. However, I used to enjoy dancing as a young kid and I even participated in dance contests, soul train lines and talent show choreography. As a teen playing trumpet in my R&B band, I used to do steps and movement to the songs we played. I truly believe that all of that activity contributed to my ability to make beats and improvise rhythms. I encourage you to move your body to the rhythms and they will flow easier through you.

Be Willing to Do the Grunt Work

Learn how to rap. I know I lost a lot of you with that one. I am serious, though. You should take one of your favorite rap songs and learn how to rap the lyrics exactly the way the rapper did it. Imitate every breath the rapper takes, every change in vocal pitch they make, and every grunt you hear. I used to love the Melle Mel grunts like "Ah Rrrruh!" The sound of his voice and grunts were as important to the rap as the lyrics themselves. I learned how to listen to this quality from listening to the entire repertoire of James Brown. Every sound he made was magical. I loved how he changed his voice from song to song, and how he emphasized hits, screams, and squeals. Learn the differences between rappers' phrasings and their accents. Digital Underground's "Humpty Dance," Eminem's "Slim Shady," Tone Loc's "Wild Thing," LL Cool J's "I Need Love," Ice Cube's "Today Was a Good Day," Mystikal's "Shake Ya Ass," and Tupac's "Keep Your Head Up" all possess totally different rap sounds and feels. You must use your ears to learn how to articulate those kinds of differences. It is a challenge, but a necessary one if you expect to create beats.

Spoons, Hambone, and Hoofing

Traditionally, African American music included the use of drums and percussion as the core instruments used to create songs. During the enslavement period in early America (from the 1600s to reconstruction in the 1880s), African Americans used African drums, congas, and other percussion to create beats. During the early years of slavery, African people in America were prohibited from using drums or speaking their native languages. This quickly led to the African American making do with ordinary utensils and household items such as washtub bass, washboards, guitars, kettles, and spoons in order to make beats. Notably, this lead to the creation of other commensurate styles such as Caribbean steel drum music, bluegrass, and blues.

During the enslavement process, African Americans would develop a kind of hand technique commonly called **juba pattin'**. This is the practice of playing hand rhythms on the chest or legs, and developed within the New Orleans/Mississippi Delta region during the enslavement era. Many African Americans used *pattin'* as a form of entertainment or as a way of passing the time. Being from St. Louis myself, as a kid, pattin' was quite common. Out of this pattin' came a specific syncopated pattern that required the person pattin' to use their ears, hands, shoulders, and feet in a particularly difficult way. This pattern was called the **hambone**. A hambone is a type of rhythm pattern played with the hands on various parts of the body in order to make music. A shuffle-type rhythm is commonly played on the chest, lap, or stomach, and employs both sides (front and back) of the hands to achieve variables of syncopation and accents within the pattern. A well-known song called "Hambone" was created to sing along with the rhythm. Jazz artist Bobby McFerrin is known for his expertise with hambone and other rhythms. Throughout African musical history there are documented occurrences of specific rhythms being executed uniformly by vocalists or musicians.

Once a person learned the hambone correctly, that person could make beats and establish a good back beat with which others could sing, dance, and rhyme with. This type of dance and pattin' technique has evolved into stomp routines like the ones we see on schoolyards, college fraternities, and big-time Broadway musical productions. Although many people are credited for the hambone, it was Bo Diddley who brought out the essence of this rhythm in his early rock 'n' roll/R&B songs. There was no mistaking his preach-style rap/singing and influence on the young dancers of his day.

In addition to the use of rhythms with homemade instruments and hambone rhythms were the different types of **foot dances** that developed. These foot dances were developed specifically for the purpose of creating rhythmic sounds to be used to make beats. From before the days of early tap or soft shoe came the practice of laying a thin board (usually made of plywood) on a hard surface such as the floor or ground.

The board was then sprinkled with salt. Next, dancers began using the heel of the shoe and slide effect from the toe on the salt to make beats. Once African Americans were allowed to wear shoes, the salt was replaced with metal taps on both heel and toe of the shoe. This act was seen and compared to the same practice as nailing or shoeing a metal plate on the hoof of a horse, and thus came the idea of **hoofing**. With hoofing, the dancers would make beats within the structure of various song forms. Interestingly, many of these tap rhythms are the same ones used on the kick, hi-hat, and snare patterns heard on contemporary Hip-Hop songs.

The next few examples are presented for you to listen to and emulate. The parts you play are either piano or string parts. Each example contains very syncopated drum rhythms that can be felt while playing your part. Be careful to not lose time when listening to the drum parts.

These rhythms and beats are designed to be imitated. They are common Hip-Hop beats which you should memorize and internalize. Once you get a handle on the feel and execution, begin beat boxing and even try to hambone some of these patterns.

If necessary, just sing or play one of the rhythms first. If this is still too difficult, move your body to the beat and clap your hands on beats 2 and 4. This will serve as a marker for your growth as you continue to practice these patterns throughout this book.

Scrub A Dub

TRACK 15

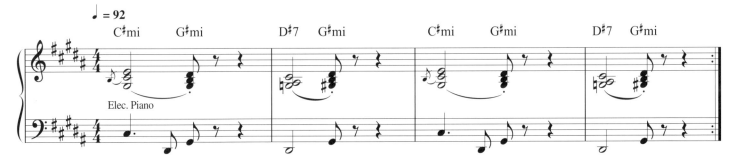

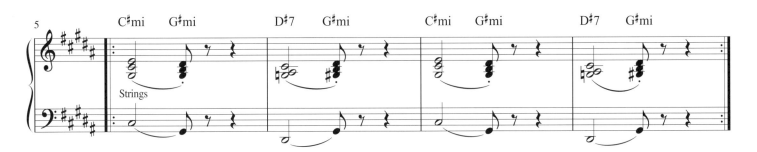

Married Slow

TRACK 16

Extra Facts

TRACK 17

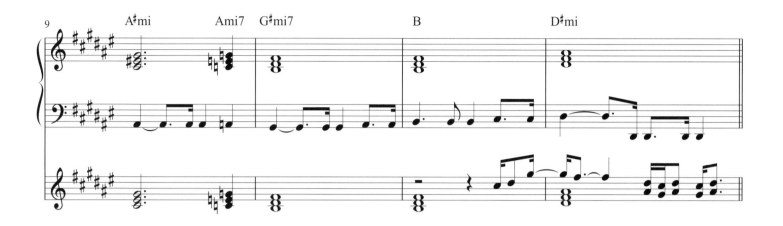

Boy She Is Fine

TRACK 18

Every Ting

TRACK 19

Wildin' Out

TRACK 20

Techno Hop 1

TRACK 21

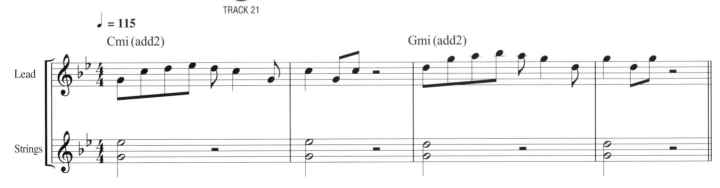

Chapter Four

4 BUSTIN' RHYMES, HITS, AND BASS LINES

In this chapter we will begin to examine the ideas behind rhymes, hits (accents), and bass lines, all of which contribute to the melodic flow of the music. These ideas make up the anatomy of Hip-Hop's most basic components. Much of Hip-Hop is and has always been centered on the rap or the rhyme itself. We will take a closer look into its most vital organs which are none other than rhythm & rhyme! There is a natural rhythm to every verbal phrase that anyone utters. If you say or recite a phrase with the right tempo, placement, and accent, then your message becomes elucidated. Conversely, if you speak too slowly, hesitate in your delivery, or mumble the words, your message will not be communicated effectively, nor will it be received well. When this rhythm is performed effectively with a natural chain of ideas presented with just the right emphasis and meaning, a poet or speaker reaches subconscious awareness. This type of performance is known as **prose**. The delivery is essential in the effect of prose on one's audience! In other words, there is a musical time and place for everything, and unless you are in tune to the natural flow of music, you will find yourself playing outside of the groove.

Poetically speaking, a rhyme is a word that phonetically sounds like another word. The words *stone* and *bone* both sound alike, but have different meanings. If I said, "I'll take this stone and hit you with it, then your bone will be broken," I am not using the rhyme words effectively. However, if I said, "I dug for a bone, but I came up with a stone," then that is a correct way to utilize the rhyme. When we rhyme, we put words into an order that will result in the rhyming word stated last. This produces a resolution or cadence to our phrase. Simply put, a Hip-Hop rhyme is a pattern of words put together in a rhythm that produces auditory symmetry. When we hear the rhyme, it evokes motion in our senses and gives us space to comprehend words, and depth in which to perceive the message of each phrase clearly.

Musically speaking, while playing your keyboard parts you must keep in mind how it fits within the groove. It's gotta rhyme too! A groove is a rhythmic pattern played by different instruments in a fashion that locks the parts together. You must stay aware of each part rhythmically, harmonically, melodically and tonally. This is something that takes a great deal of time to learn and execute, but when it is done efficiently it is magical.

Just Looking for (TLC) Tagging, Limericks, and Childhood

Graffiti is the act of writing phrases, names, symbols, and images on the wall. This act is usually seen as derogatory because of the language used and the affiliation with gangs marking their territory as a way of *staking out* (claiming ownership of) neighborhoods. Some see this as street art and have dubbed it *tagging*. This act is further misunderstood because of the lack of respect of taggers defacing private property. Ultimately, the tagger is someone who is identifying with the need to express their childhood repressions. These are the people whose stories aren't being heard, but they are telling their story on the wall. A wise person is one who can *read the writing on the wall*. This type of art or use of symbols as language can be interpreted as an artistic expression. The walls of Egyptian temples are filled with this type of art.

Historically, poetry has taken on several types of forms. Some of these forms have been named *odes*, *sonnets*, or *quatrains*. One such form is called a **limerick**. A limerick is a very old type of five-lined poem. Its form quickly tells a story and usually ends with a humorous punch line. In literal poetic structure, different types of poems are labeled based on their particular use of patterns and rhymes. Funk master George Clinton used this device on many improvisations of his songs like "Undisco Kidd" and "Supergroovalisticprosifunkstication!"

The different rhythms and cadences used in these various forms of poetry are how we define the structure itself. Rap and Hip-Hop routinely use all of these forms of poetry. This is achieved through multiple syncopated and rapid-fire lyrical twists and turns. In other words, the rapper improvises or "free-styles" until he/she stumbles upon some or all of these patterns. Listen to the rhythm and rhyme of rap lyrics to see how many poetic forms you can hear. Do you notice the symmetry?

Another clue to the validity of Hip-Hop's close relationship to childhood is its common use of school-yard rhymes in rap lyrics. When I was a young child in St. Louis, Missouri, I would often see school girls rapping. Some of the most common traditional raps were "Miss Lucy Had a Baby" and "Oh Mary Mack" (Babyface recorded this eminent domain classic in 1986). Little girls would jump rope or play hopscotch, paddle ball, or jacks while singing rhymes like "One Two Buckle My Shoe," or "Hickory Dickory Dock." The song "369-Goose Drank Wine" used to be one of my favorite childhood raps. St. Louis rapper Nelly recorded a huge hit with "Country Grammar," which was a combination of school-yard rhymes heard on the streets for a hundred years or more. Jay-Z's "Hard Knock Life," taken from the popular children's musical *Annie*, is another example. The recently released 2006 "Chain Hang Low" by the artist Jibbs, which was taken from the children's classic "Do Your Ears Hang Low," demonstrates this childhood Hip-Hop connection perfectly!

I Need Those Hits

A **hit** is a musical accent in most African American musical genres designed to act as period or exclamation point so as to *button* a phrase or melodic idea. James Brown is the origina-tor of the slang term, *hit*. It can be done with any instrument or sound, but it is often done with synthesizers, strings, horns, crash cymbals, or other loud and dynamic instruments. A hit can be achieved with the entire band attacking a unison note and glissing (falling or sliding) off the notes. Another more common instrument associated with hits in Hip-Hop is a sampler. A sample hit can be anything, any sound or any effect.

A sample hit can be a vocal yell, an explosion, or even synthetic ambience. James Brown used hits extensively in all of his songs. This made for a dramatic effect when he changed verses, choruses, and even when he changed songs.

Hits have to be played with just the right finesse and attitude so as to produce the desired result in the music. Remember that hits should accent the music, so if you play too many, or

James Brown

Photo: Paul Bergen, Redferns Music Picture Library

bury the drums or the rap with hits, they will loose their emphasis. Some Hip-Hop songs that utilize hits are "8th Wonder" by the Sugarhill Gang, "The Message" by Grandmaster Flash & the Furious Five, "The Show" by Doug E. Fresh, Houdini's "Friends," and the LA Dream Team's "Dream Team Is in the House." Almost all rap songs have hits, and they have become a characteristic within the Hip-Hop genre.

Cut the Bass Up

The bass line has become the single most important ingredient in Hip-Hop music. It is paramount as the defining part of a Hip-Hop song. One of the reasons for this is that early disco dictated that bass parts should be repetitive. In some cases it was the only way one could tell the difference from one song to another. In disco songs, drum parts were very similar to each other, and tempos were anchored at 120 bpm. The bass melody became the life's blood of the disco song. No matter what string or horn arrangement you sweetened the song with, the bass part remained simple and identifiable.

Since Hip-Hop was an extension of disco, it stands to reason that the need for a strong and solid bass line would be the foundation of Hip-Hop. There are many songs that demonstrate this fact. The songs "White Lines" by Grandmaster Flash & Melle Mel and "White Horse" by Laid Back both have strong bass lines.

In the mid 1980s many Hip-Hop songs took on a techno sound and flavor as stated earlier. The bass guitar sound was often replaced by a bass synthesizer. The Moog Minimoog keyboard had always been the instrument of choice for funky and low bass sounds. There were many others however, such as the ARP Odyssey, Roland Jupiter, and the Yamaha DX7 which could do a professional job.

The bass sounds on these synthesizers are now vintage sounds that can be purchased as virtual instruments in the form of computer software programs. It might be a good idea to familiarize yourself with those older sounds as well as current bass sounds, since they are such a huge part of Hip-Hop.

The bass is an instrument that must be played solidly in time with the drum groove. It requires great focus and creativity in order to make a bass part fit like a glove without changing the feel throughout the entire song. It has to have enough presence and life so as to not get boring, without losing time or being too busy. If you have ever recorded bass parts, you are aware of just how tricky it is to make the parts stick.

An important aspect of understanding bass from a keyboard player's perspective is to know the range of a bass guitar. Many of the early Hip-Hop songs included real electric bass, and in order to play this type of bass correctly you must know the notes on the bass guitar neck. In fact, you should know how a bass guitar is tuned. A standard four-string bass guitar has a low E string followed by A, D, and G strings above. If you were trying to emulate a five-string bass guitar, you would include an extra low B string that is even lower than the E string on the four-string bass. Another idea is to use a synthesizer that has fret noises sampled on different keys of your keyboard. With these extra effects you can imitate the slides, thumps, and plucks that a real bass player can play. You may also want to get familiar with some of the effect pedals and amp settings that bass players like to use.

The hits and bass lines presented as examples in this chapter will familiarize you with common Hip-Hop bass lines and give you an opportunity to play one un-quantized. Be sure to lock in as solidly as possible with the drum. Bear in mind that if a rapper were on these tracks you would have to preserve space for the rap rhythm, so don't overplay.

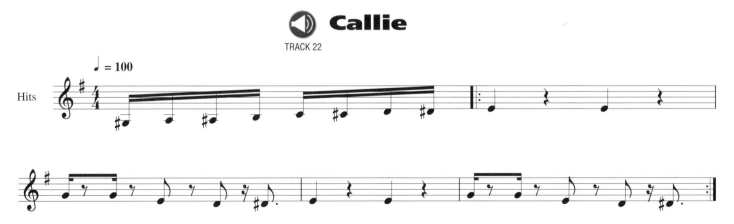

Pump It

TRACK 23

Rain Water

TRACK 24

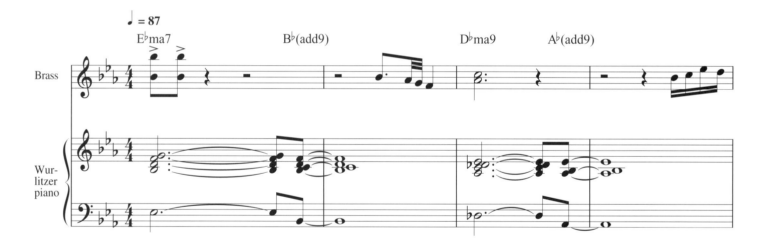

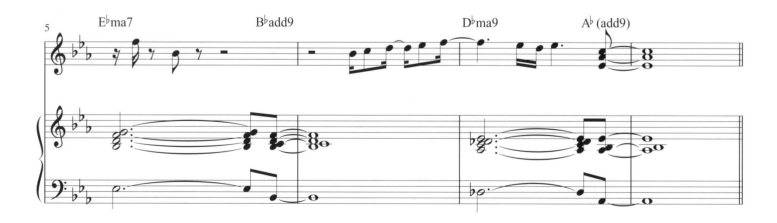

Big Phattie

TRACK 25

Hip Bass 1

TRACK 26

Hip Bass 2

TRACK 27

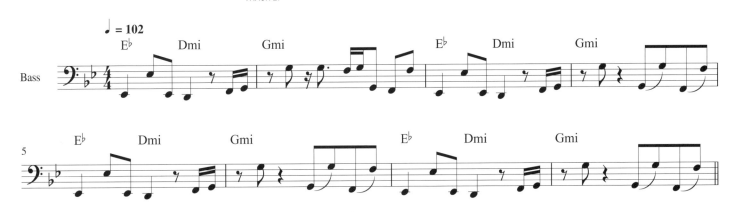

Hip Bass 3

TRACK 28

Slippery Hop

TRACK 29

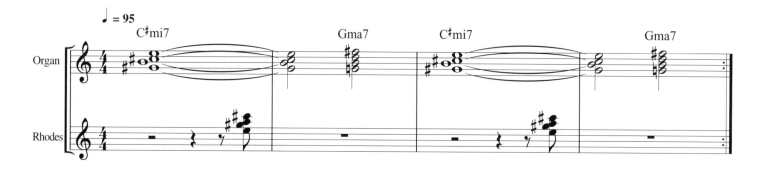

Chapter Five

5

NEW JACK SWING

Hip-Hop began a new era of rhythms, sounds, and grooves after it reached huge success in the late 1980s. Hip-Hop records were dominating African American radio and the dance clubs were filled with young people dancing to the latest funky rap repertoire. But things were becoming predictable. Even though Hip-Hop was danceable, it lacked the melodic touch that R&B had with its plethora of soul singers. Record companies were looking for young acts who could sing but still keep the sensibilities of the Hip-Hop community. There were singers on records, but not enough of them exhibited vocal skills that companies could rely on for hit after hit.

On the east coast in New Jersey in the late 1980s, a singing group emerged and began touring the country billed as a new Jackson 5. The group had five singers who were great dancers, entertainers, and best of all they could also rap. These young men were known as New Edition. Produced by local producer and manager Maurice Starr, the group spiraled to fame and stardom. They featured future stars Ricky Bell, Michael Bivins, Bobby Brown, Ralph Tresvant, and Ronnie DeVoe. This group would later add R&B singer Johnny Gill when Bobby Brown went solo, and Bell, Bivins, and DeVoe (BBD) would later score a huge hit with the dance-inspired song "Poison." New Edition began to bring exciting, new, and faster rhythms to Hip-Hop. Needless to say, they garnered huge success and were the predecessors of the popular group Boyz II Men.

As mentioned earlier, R&B and rap dance songs often consisted of triplet-styled shuffle rhythms that grooved with the type of syncopation that dancers love. Eddie Kendricks' "Keep On Truckin'" is a great example of these triplet or *swing* rhythms that include hits and break downs in its song arrangement. Many of the songs from the early 1990s contained swing rhythms such as this. These elements are a cross fusion of drum rhythms previously introduced in blues, jazz, Latin, and R&B. By the early 1990s, digital recordings captured the full force of these powerful drum sounds and sizzling hi-hat patterns. The piano sound was becoming popular again because of the influence of the vocalists. In short, the time was ripe for the second phase of the growth of Hip-Hop.

Another group of singers to come along during this time would be the catalyst to set Hip-Hop on fire. This group featured a trio of performers whose keyboard player was the group's leader, songwriter, and producer. The group was called Guy, and the keyboard player was Teddy Riley. As a musician Teddy Riley clearly was influenced by the go-go music from the D.C. area. Many of his group's percussion patterns were commonly used in go-go. Teddy's first huge successful work was done in 1985 with Slick Rick and Doug E. Fresh.

New Jack Swing is a hybrid of R&B and Hip-Hop that began between the late 1980s and mid 1990s. It is a mixture of soulful lush lead and background harmonies à la Stevie Wonder and Charlie Wilson, along with heavy swing rhythms and urban powerful backbeats. It often contained hits and squeals commonly heard in rap and Hip-Hop music. New Jack Swing is characterized by triplet patterns that lend themselves to rappers and dancers. Its influence gave R&B artists easy passage into the world of Hip-Hop.

Teddy and his heavy synthesizer work, which was present on all the Guy records like *Groove Me, Teddy's Jam*, and *I Like*, gained fame and sold millions of records. Additionally, Teddy redefined the Hip-Hop sound with his self-titled New Jack Swing sound. Teddy is known for his discovery of Pharrell Williams and Chad Hugo who comprise the Neptunes. As a successful R&B/Hip-Hop producer, Teddy produced many artists including Aaron Hall's solo CDs (Guy's lead singer). Teddy formed and produced two other successful groups called Wreckx-N-Effect, who had a major hit with "Rump Shaker," and Blackstreet, who recorded the huge hit "No Diggity." Teddy performed all of the funky keyboard work on these albums. Other hits produced by Teddy include Michael Jackson's "Jam" and "Remember the Time" from his *Dangerous* CD.

In the 1990s many artists came on the scene performing New Jack Swing. Songs like Tony Terry's "When I'm with You," Bobby Brown's "My Prerogative," Johnny Kemp's "Just Got Paid," Heavy D's "Overweight Lover," and Color Me Badd's "I Wanna Sex You Up" were all New Jack Swing hits.

Veteran producer Babyface dabbled in the New Jack Swing style with hits he produced like "Girlfriend" and "Mercedes Boy" by Pebbles, and "Superwoman" by Karyn White. Babyface was a huge influence on Hip-Hop, even though he was primarily an R&B/pop songwriter and producer. Even though these songs contained no rap, they were still popular within the Hip-Hop genre. Other artists like Levert ("Cassanova"), Keith Sweat ("I Want Her") and C+C Music Factory ("Gonna Make You Sweat") used heavy New Jack Swing rhythms as a foundation for their grooves.

Hip-Hop on TV and Films

With the huge success of Hip-Hop and the direction change of New Jack Swing, the television and motion picture industries took notice of the upcoming rappers and producers. Rap already had films created around the genre like *Beat Street, Breakin' 1 & 2, Krush Groove* and many others. Now films like *New Jack City, The Show, Wild Style, Fear of a Black Hat, Boyz N the Hood, Menace to Society, 8 Mile* (starring Eminem who received an Oscar in 2002 for Best Song with "Lose Yourself"), *Hustle & Flow* (soundtrack with Three 6 Mafia and artist Terrence Howard; received an Oscar for Best Song with "It's Hard Out Here for a Pimp" in 2006), Spike Lee's *Bamboozled*, and many others have been filmed, and of course, more are on the way.

Rappers turned actors Queen Latifah, Ice-T, LL Cool J, Ice Cube, Snoop Dogg, Mos Def, Ludacris, and many others have dozens of film credits.

On television, "Fresh Prince of Bel Air" featured Will Smith and DJ Jazzy Jeff as actors; "Living Single" featured Queen Latifah; "In the House" featured LL Cool J; and Lil' Romeo is the star of his self-titled cable TV show. Many other Hip-Hop artists have been featured on VH-1, MTV, BET, and prime time TV shows. I must not exclude Flava Flav's hit reality shows "Flavor of Love" and "Strange Love" featuring actress Brigitte Nielsen.

It was during the mid to late 1990s that Hip-Hop began to bling. Gold chains were at a premium and money was there to be made. Hip-Hop had reached its *Golden Age*. Rapper MC Hammer, starting his career in Oakland, California in 1987, spearheaded this golden age of Hip-Hop. Stanley "Hammer" Burrell, with his monster hit "U Can't Touch This," catapulted his status to mainstream artist in the early 1990s. His elaborate stage shows and dazzling clothes, electrifying dance moves and his army of entourages led the way for mega Hip-Hop acts of today!

MC Hammer

The Deep Groove Hip-Hop Influence

Deep Groove is an approach to performing Hip-Hop music on radio and in clubs. In the 1990s it became common practice for DJs to cross-fade one track into the next. This practice produced a sort of seamless way of changing from one song to the other without losing time or talking. It was especially effective on the radio because a DJ could compress all the tempos to 100 bpm and fade continuously between songs without ever stopping. In the club, the DJ could keep all of the dancers on the floor. In addition to the nuance of party effect, this deep groove would produce some interesting musical results such as hearing Queen's "Another One Bites the Dust" with the drum and bass line of Chic's "Good Times"! A good example of the deep groove effect is on the song "Grandmaster Flash on the Wheels of Steel" by Grandmaster Flash.

In order for this effect to work, songs had to have the funky bass, slammin' backbeat, and repetitive melodies and lyrics that would lend themselves to this approach. R&B and funk songs like "Dazz" by Brick, "Doin' Da Butt" by E.U., and many others served as the template grooves for dozens to come. The deep groove influence on these songs spawned copy-cat songs like "Me, Myself & I" by De La Soul (Parliament's "Knee Deep"), "I'm a Slave 4 You" by Britney Spears (Vanity 6's "Nasty Girls"), and Ashanti and Ja Rule's "Happy" (The Gap Band's "Outstanding").

Some current deep groove tunes include "Too Close" and "Wifey" by Next, "Home Alone" by R. Kelly and Keith Murray, "Let's Get Down" by Tony Toni Tone and DJ Quik, "Get Your Freak On" by Missy Elliott, and "Sexy Back" by Justin Timberlake.

It is important to note that many rap and Hip-Hop artists throughout the 1990s and early 2000s performed heavy dance-influenced grooves. Like the genesis of Hip-Hop, the beat and the music were the true inspiration for most of these artists. Emphasis on just having fun, as well as a party atmosphere, became crucial for this type of *deep groove!* Most artists had danceable Hip-Hop tracks, but certain artists strayed away from the stereotypical rap messages and stuck to the rhythmic babble of the DJ roots. In other words, they gave their audiences uncut heavy deep groove. Some of these deep groove Hip-Hop artists included the Sugarhill Gang, Grandmaster Flash & the Furious Five, MC Hammer, Young MC ("Bust a Move"), Lighter Shade of Brown, Coolio, Digable Planets, Digital Underground, Kid 'N Play, Salt-N-Peppa, Montell Jordan, Tupac, DJ Quik, and many others.

The following examples are grooves and patterns representing the new influence of New Jack Swing grooves. Be careful to interpret these rhythms with the triplet and shuffle 16th notes that were common with this style. Also be sure to articulate the rhythms cleanly so as to sit "in the pocket" like the drum pattern does. Remember to listen to the recordings alluded to in this chapter. When you listen with a purpose, it helps you to play these patterns with much more authority and, of course, with the right attitude.

🔊 New Jack Pizzaz

TRACK 30

Playin' & Kiddin'

TRACK 31

Swing 16ths ♩ = 103

Cruel Jack

TRACK 32

Swing 16ths ♩ = 110

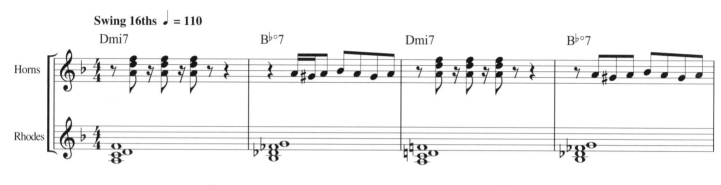

Dollar Bills

TRACK 33

Swing 16ths ♩ = 108

DJ Break 1

TRACK 34

DJ Break 2

TRACK 35

Chapter Six

6 SAMPLING, SQUEALS, AND SCRATCHES

This chapter will address some of the technical issues of recording samples that are commonly used in Hip-Hop. Because of the nature of the technical jargon associated with this type of music production, it is advised that you research and study electronic music. There are many books, articles, and videos currently on the market to enhance your knowledge in this area. A modest crash course of sorts may help you to understand the basic premise of this discussion.

A **sample** is a digitally recorded event. The event could be anything from music previously recorded to sound effects you are currently recording with a microphone. The word "event" is more appropriate than "recording" because the recording process is done with data rather than imprinting signal codes on a tape. When imprinting musical signal codes in numeric data codes (like a computer processor), the data recorded is much more accurate. In fact, when you sample a sound, it is virtually identical to the original sound, given the limitations of your bandwidth, megahertz, or processing accuracy.

Making a Hip-Hop Track

In Hip-Hop, sampling from records is a process that often occurs in the creation stages of making beats. The practice of using the machines to aid in composing began in early techno and rap music. Rap and techno almost always included some sample within the recording, and in some cases, the entire record could be a sample.

A songwriter/producer uses samples of whole drumbeats or drum sounds when composing the grooves for Hip-Hop. Some of the machines that have been used traditionally for this task were the Roland, Yamaha, Ensoniq, Korg, and Casio drum machines and keyboards. The Linn 9000 drum machine was also very popular in the early years of rap. After much scrutiny, the instrument of choice became the Akai MPC drum machine. It had the ability to record complex quantize feels, huge pads for beat programming, and universal connectivity for syncing and for SMPTE video transferring. The next step in the process was to establish some musical hook, like a bass sound or an actual prerecorded sample of a track.

Both of these options could be achieved with a sample. Samples traditionally were recorded on digital sampling keyboards, stored on a common storage medium (like disks, cassettes, or hard drives), and then mastered to digital tape (DAT) or CDs.

When a sample is created and then strung together from the end of one section (i.e., a four-bar phrase) to the start of the sample, that is called **looping**. A loop is a function that allows the sample to repeat itself. Looping a sample allows you to keep retriggering the sample throughout the song rather than storing all of that data in separate sections of the song. This loop becomes a single event, saving lots of memory space. A loop can be programmed for either infinite or designated amounts of retriggering.

Hip-Hop arrangements were often fairly sparse, so the next step would be to add the vocals to the tracks. With these parts on the recording, and well within the ear of the producer, the song idea can really begin to take shape. It is usually at this time that a producer will add the sweetening or *flava'* to augment the main parts of the track. A keyboard player would record desired parts or sounds so as to give more color to the picture that had already been painted. Sometimes this process occurs before the rapper or vocalist is recorded onto the track; however, that could lead to making the keyboard part too busy. I recommend listening to the vocal or rapper first for better results.

If and when you decide to use sample techniques, study the art of mixing and cross-fading samples into your tracks. Listen to Puffy Combs, Dr. Dre, and Rodney Jerkins for good examples.

Hip-Hop and the Computer

The processes of sampling and looping were originally performed on keyboards. They were tedious and involved: recording, layering, rendering, and saving with difficult commands, memory shortage issues, and monitoring, all this with tiny little keyboard screens and LED readouts. Needless to say, the sampling machine had to be relegated to early retirement and its sampling tasks delegated to the computer. With software programs such as Logic, Cubase, Pro Tools, Sonar, and others, you can now record a CD directly into your recorder's track. All of the editing jobs like time stretching, looping, transposing, and effecting now can be easily done with mere key strokes on a computer keypad.

Other virtual instrument software programs like Reason (a sequence software with groove pallets) and Garage Band allow you to not only sample, but make Hip-Hop beats that are legal and free to be used. This is a great option for the songwriter to make beats and not worry about copyright or mechanical right infringement.

Nowadays data storage is painless and plentiful. With gigs and gigs of hard drive space, and CD and DVD storage medium, it is a simple thing to save an entire library's worth of data. You can even opt for external data storage via USB or Firewire. Devices such as Zip, Jaz, or Lacie drives, smart media cards, memory sticks, or even your laptop computer can store your tracks, artwork, and sequence data.

Your Personal Hip-Hop Keyboards

Over the years just about every type of keyboard that was ever invented has been used in Hip-Hop and most every other style for that matter. However, there have always been instruments that appear more functional and suitable than others. For example, the Ensoniq ASR-10 used to be very inexpensive, contained a myriad of sounds, and had sequencing capabilities to utilize those sounds. It was a good choice for some musicians.

Korg Triton

The Roland Juno series keyboards have always been great for bass sounds and for getting the feel and attacks funky. In fact, Roland always had great strings and lead sounds. Yamaha drum sounds have always had that crispy tight sound that works great for Hip-Hop drum beats. Korg keyboards have great brass, strings, organs, and lead synthe-sizer sounds.

Yamaha Motif

As far as playing live, almost all Hip-Hop keyboard players prefer the sounds and the accessibility of the Korg Triton series or the Yamaha Motif series. There are great combination sounds, hybrid samples, and programmability on all of their machines. Another good option is the Roland Phantom.

The fact is, with MIDI rack mounts and weighted controllers, it is possible to use just about any instruments you want and still achieve the results you desire to recreate Hip-Hop songs live.

In the Hip-hop world, once the entire recording process was completed, the producer would print up mass quantities of dubbed CDs, artwork, and packaging, and then sell them out of the trunk of the car, on the streets, or while performing live at clubs.

Sampling Information and Informed Samplers

There is quite a lot of information to learn about the technical aspects of sampling and the legal aspects of sampling as well. Many Hip-Hop artists, songwriters, and producers have found themselves in court for using right-protected intellectual property. In short, you just can't sample anything you want and use it on your CDs with impunity. You must get prior permission, pay royalties, and give written credit on your CD to the music's rightful owners. The latest trend has been for Hip-Hop composers who use recorded samples of complete songs to re-copyright the song with the inclusion of the new writer as a new song. This serves the purpose of right-protecting any future use of that incarnation of the new recording (they still must gain permission from the original writer to use the copyrighted song). Most Hip-Hop artists now have *Sample Clearance* divisions within their organizations for just these types of matters. However, if you are an individual keyboardist/producer, you must become personally aware of these licensing issues.

In my previous books, *R&B Soul Keyboards* and *Pop Rock Keyboards* (both published by Hal Leonard Corporation), I have addressed the issue of sampling information in different chapters of each book. As stated earlier, this may require more study to fully understand exactly how to sample with a computer system. In addition to specialized books and DVDs on this subject, a private tutoring from a professional on the system that you are working with is recommended.

The informed sampler is a person who not only knows how to sample, but also what to sample. Hip-Hop is filled with songs that are revised or "souped up" versions of older songs. The real artistry is in finding and selecting which song is best suited for sampling and/or recreating. There is a skill to doing this.

An *informed sampler* is one who knew that Beyoncé's "Crazy in Love" featuring her fiancé and rap mogul Jay-Z, was sampled from the Chi-Lites' "Are You My Woman?" An informed sampler would know that Kool & the Gang's "Soul Vibrations" has been sampled as a horn fanfare for hundreds of Hip-Hop tunes. An informed sampler knows that Warren G and Nate Dogg's "Regulate" uses the rhythm section groove from Michael McDonald's (credited as composed by Lieber and Stoller) hit song "I Keep Forgetting."

One must possess an ear for sounds and putting things together with an existing beat. You must also be able to hear sounds within separate recordings and imagine what they would sound like blended together. This blending of sounds must not be obscured or buried by different ranges, tempos, or keys. This is not as simple as it may first appear to be.

Hip-Hop producers are responsible for strategically choosing certain kinds of grooves to complement their songs and connect with their listening audience. The Hip-Hop song "Back in the Day" was recorded by Ahmad in 1994. It used the track from a Teddy Pendergrass R&B classic, "Love TKO," as its hook. The song "O.P.P." by Naughty By Nature used the Jackson 5's "ABC" for its hook. Rap veteran Rob Base used the James Brown classic "Think" (as performed by Lynn Collins) as the hook for his "It Takes Two" dance hit. Will Smith's "Summertime" was originally Kool & the Gang's "Summer Madness." Coolio used Stevie Wonder's "Pastime Paradise" for the hook of his monster hit "Gangsta's Paradise," and rapper Too Short recreated Donny Hathaway's smash hit "The Ghetto." There are dozens of examples of this common approach where sampling creatively results in big hits.

An even more challenging effort is to try to select effects, riffs, and licks from existing songs and rip them into your Hip-Hop track. In this method, the new use of the riff or lick is often entirely different from its original use. Keyboard players will often have to assume arrangement tasks and make production decisions in Hip-Hop, and you may be required to develop this skill. In order to master this, it is suggested you try listening to Hip-Hop songs and determine which CDs the horn lines, bass licks, vocal snippets, drum beats, and guitar-licks come from. Is this really possible? The informed sampler can do it, so the answer is yes.

Squeals

A **squeal** is a relatively new concept in musical orchestration and is unique to Hip-Hop. It is a sonic ambience made up of a central melodic idea that is *pedal pointed* (a musical element such as a drone that continues steadily in a song while other elements change) throughout the song. It is usually a sample of some hyped section in a song such as an intro, solo, or break section. The synthesizer solo on the Ohio Player's "Funky Worm" is a universally used squeal. Another common squeal is the saxophone (Coltrane-like) squeal heard on the beginning of the song "The Grunt" by James Brown's band The JBs. Some squeals' origins are not known. In fact, a clever producer purposely camouflages his/her original squeals. The guitar-like squeal used on Erykah Badu's "Bag Lady" and several gangsta rap hits is a great example of a camouflaged squeal.

Most squeals are synthetic in tone quality and tend to have a thin metallic piercing sound. The first squeal I heard on a Hip-Hop record was a long ascending synthesizer glide effect. I don't recall what CD it was, but after that it has appeared countless times on many other recordings including Public Enemy's "Fight the Power." Since it is usually sampled from some other recording, it carries with it ambience from that recording. Technically speaking, this can be considered as noise, from an engineer's perspective.

Other types of squeals include vocalisms like the James Brown screams and grunts used on Rob Base's "It Takes Two." Nonetheless, a squeal serves as Hip-Hop vibe for most producers. This added hype noise is also called *racket*. We will visit this idea in the next chapter.

A good example of a squeal being used in a Hip-Hop song is Quincy Jones' "Back on the Block," with the squeal taken from Quincy's "Theme from Ironside." Another example is Usher's (featuring Lil' Jon & Ludacris) "Yeah," where nearly every part of the song is a squeal. Bone Thugs-N-Harmony's "Thuggish Ruggish Bone" also has multiple squeals. Missy Elliott's "Get Your Freak On" also uses a rhythmic and melodic squeal. The new Ciara's latest song "Goodies" features a gliding squeal.

Scratches

The word **scratch** refers to the sound that the vinyl recording makes when the needle of the turntable hits the record. Since the power of the amplifier is on, when listening to the record, a brief scrunch sound occurs when the needle lands. This sound is also heard when inaccurately sliding the needle point on the surface of the recording. When this happens, the record grooves can be slightly scarred or altered. If the grooves are no longer seamless and smooth, then the needle will fail to rotate to the next groove in line. If that happens, the recording will play in the same groove it played in its previous revolution. The result is a repeat of the same section of a recording. This is what is known as a broken or *scratched* record. This scratch surprisingly produces unusual and interesting results. A new song idea can come from a record scratch effect.

DJs, or disc jockeys, found this effect very musical. They also found the sound of the needle hitting the record musical as well. They began purposely sliding their hands in a rhythmic fashion producing a hype sound used to punctuate song ideas. Since DJs always had multiple copies of hit records and unlimited access to accessories such as extra turntable needles, they were willing to bang up a few records and needles for the sake of a hyped performance. It worked like a charm and the rest is history!

There are all sorts of great DJs that are infamous for their great spinning and selection of records. Nearly all the DJs in New York City and the Bronx from the early rap years until now have set the trend for spinning. Grandmaster Flash is probably the world's greatest DJ/spinner, and set into motion the DJ-as-creator idea. Of all the DJs in Hip-Hop, few can argue that the late great Jam Master Jay from Run-DMC was the most famous. His work on the classic smash hit "King of Rock," along with his visible presence in the movie *Krush Groove*, gave him star status. His high profile gave new glory to the DJ. Keyboard players in this style must work closely with the DJ both live and in the studio.

The combination of samples, hits, squeals, and scratches are the responsibilities of the keyboard player and the DJ. If you are the only keyboard player, then you have your work cut out for you. If you are working with a DJ in a live situation, then the two of you must assign and share duties. It behooves you to study the work of DJs like Jam Master Jay and others. Jay even has a video currently on the market on the subject of mix mastery.

The following examples utilize samples, squeals, and scratches. The hits you hear complement the arrangement, but you should just focus on your parts. Use the sounds on your synthesizer or sampler closest to the ones being used on these CD tracks. The point is to

Grandmaster Flash

simulate the sound, feel, and rhythmic placement on each example. As you continue to work with these patterns, you will begin to see the relationship with patterns you hear on actual Hip-Hop songs.

Zoom A Zoom

TRACK 36

It's All Goody

TRACK 37

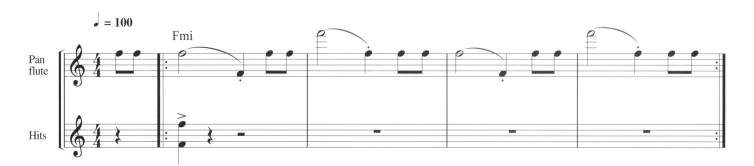

Slow Yo Roll

TRACK 38

DJ Break 3

TRACK 39

Topping the News

The following CD examples (Tracks 40–43) are from a sample of a Hip-Hop groove called "Topping the News" that I recorded some years ago for my book *R&B Soul Keyboards*. This song was created completely with sampled sounds. I recorded the original tracks on an Ensoniq ASR-10 sampler and used record vinyl ambience, vocal snippets, and scratch sounds mixed in. I have illustrated and presented the track in pieces on individual CD tracks. Listen for the *original raw sample*, the *clip and cut with bad loop*, the *finished version with smooth loop*, and a *single sample ("Go")*, which have been lifted from the track. My good friend, guitarist Gary Solt, was the musical surgeon on this track.

The following illustrations are pictures of wave files taken from "Topping the News." Observe the shape, cut points, and finished views of the samples lifted from this track. Hip-Hop keyboard players can perform these functions either directly on their sampling workstations or on a computer with audio recording-functioning software.

 Original Raw Sample

TRACK 40

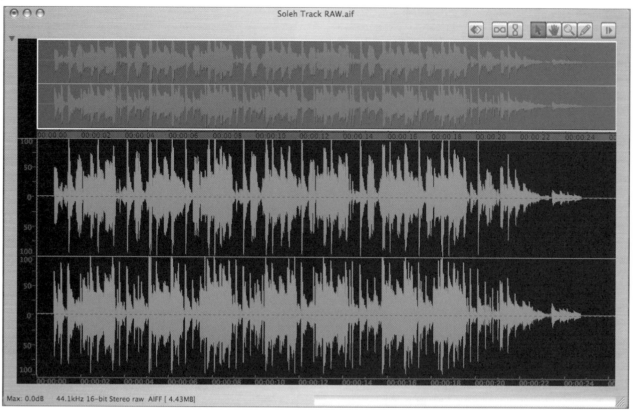

 Clip and Cut with Bad Loop

TRACK 41

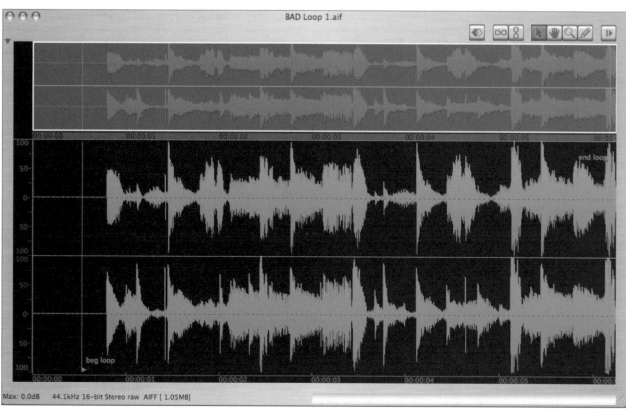

Finished Version with Smooth Loop

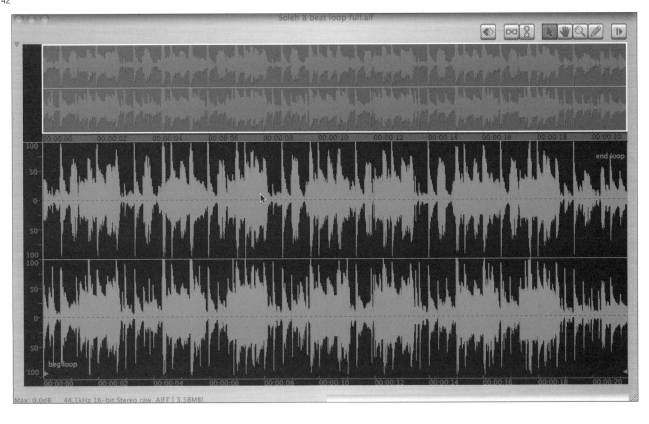

 Single Sample ("Go")

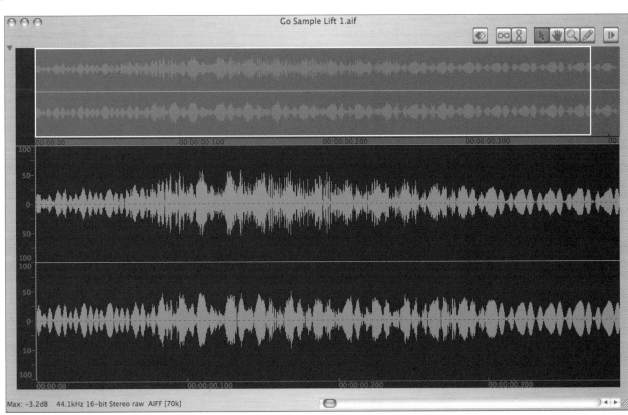

This next track features several examples of assorted racket.

 Assorted Samples, Hits, and Squeals (Triton/Motif)

TRACK 44

 **Worm & Trout Fish**

TRACK 45

Chapter Seven

7 GANGSTA GROOVE AND HIP-HOP AMBIENCE

Pimps like the author Iceberg Slim, jailhouse philosophers, and streetwise comedians were widely known for their clever anecdotes and skits describing life in the ghetto—however, they were not rappers. Comedian Rudy Ray Moore was the self-proclaimed originator of Gangsta Rap. Even though nearly all comedians used foul language in their comedy routines, he was the very first to rap about it. In the 1960s he was selling rap recordings that included music segments, and even featured these recordings in his very own movie productions. As his self-made character Dolemite, Moore rapped about his sexual prowess, his ability to administer ass kickings, his endless supply of money, and his outstanding wardrobe. This sums up the importance of the image of a gangster rapper. Since I have no intention of glorifying gangsters, I will focus on the relevance of what I call *Gangsta Groove*.

In the late 1980s and early 1990s a phenomenon was growing in Hip-Hop. More and more rappers were using explicit language and subject matter in their rap songs. Topics ranging from sex, drugs, gang violence, murder, homophobia, and racism were being commonly rapped about. From this diversion of subject matter came a new heavier brand of hardcore rap. Many rappers and their audiences sought dirtier, funkier, and even nastier grooves and lyrics.

Rapper Luther Campbell (known as Luke Skyywalker) and his group 2 Live Crew were one of the first to tour with rated X rap shows. In the mid to late 1980s, his onstage sexual antics were controversial and were often banned from certain cities. In spite of this, the group was very successful and had hit songs such as "Nasty as You Wanna Be" and "Me So Horny." Contemporary female Hip-Hop artists who followed this trend of using sexually explicit lyrics included rappers Lil' Kim, Trina, and Foxy Brown. Although rappers MC Lyte and Yo-Yo were not known as Gangsta Rappers, they each recorded Gangsta flavored Hip-Hop tracks.

Photo: Mick Hutson, Redferns Music Picture Library

Ice Cube

As rap moved to the west coast, artists like the World Class Wreckin' Cru, Schoolly D, and Too Short were making noise. Niggaz With Attitude (or N.W.A., featuring Ice Cube), Dr. Dre, and Eazy-E became huge, and were selling millions of records. Of course, it is also well-known that each member of this group went on to huge success as a solo act, even after the demise of the group.

The Beastie Boys (probably the first white rap group) recorded "You've Got to Fight (For Your Right to Party)" and went on to become very successful. Other acts like Geto Boys, the D.O.C., and many others were also selling records like crazy.

What Is Gangsta Groove?

Gangsta groove is a kind of slow grinding funky groove that has tremendous low end to it. It is weighty and heavy-to-the-floor kind of music with a powerful backbeat rhythm. Listen to James Brown's "The Payback" and you will hear all of the root elements of gangsta groove. It feels almost like the rhythm is dragging behind. Speaking musically, it has a dark and mostly minor sound to it, often containing guitar blues-lick samples, timpani rolls, bells, gongs, reverse cymbals, and arco-like string patterns. Beats 2 and 4 of the backbeat rhythm are almost always emphasized by loud cracks of handclaps. Another great example of the gangsta handclap sound can be heard on Digital Underground's "Humpty Dance." This sound was created originally by funk veteran and legend George Clinton. Clinton was the leader and mastermind of the funk groups Parliament and Funkadelic. His music and stage shows were vividly gangsta styled. He openly glorified the drug life-style. His repertoire was pretty much the soundtrack for weed parties, especially on stage during the ole school P-Funk days. Just listen to Parliament's "Flashlight" or "Aqua Boogie" and you will hear some of the characteristics of gangsta groove.

Political Rap

Some rap artists used gangsta groove to emphasize their message and didn't mind using hardcore rap concepts to do it. Even though some could be categorized as gangsta rappers, their social commentary gave them a slightly broader marketability. Some of these artists like Boogie Down Productions featuring KRS-One, Tupac, Nas, Ice-T, and X-Klan recorded rap songs that included acceptable social values.

The group Public Enemy, featuring rappers Chuck D and Flava Flav, were without a doubt the best political rap group ever recorded. They were edgy and to the street. Their lyrics of racial consciousness were fearless and they were accepted by even white audiences for their uncompromising songs. They recorded a CD called *Fear of a Black Planet* which has now become a million-selling classic. Their hit song "Fight the Power" was featured in the Spike Lee classic film, *Do the Right Thing*. Another powerful artist known for political rap was Sister Souljah. Artists like Arrested Development featuring Speech, A Tribe Called Quest, Common, Kanye West, Mos Def, and Talib Kweli are carrying on this tradition of conscious Hip-Hop.

It is notable that during the height of the gang-banging era of Hip-Hop, the most famous rappers pulled their efforts together for the cause. East Coast rappers recorded a unity song called "Self Destruction," and the West Coast rappers followed with "We're All in the Same Gang." These two recordings helped curb some of the senseless violence in the hood, and began to help turn young minds around from gang life.

The Rise of Gangsta Rap

Gangsta Rap record companies like Death Row Records in Los Angeles and Bad Boy Records in New York City were producing many rap artists and grossing nearly a billion dollars. Rap had evolved into big business. Artist Biggie Smalls (a.k.a. Notorious B.I.G.) had reached gangsta status, and his mob-styled shooting death contributed to that lore. Even the rap executives were labeled with the gangsta image. Former Death Row Records president Suge Knight had known gangster feuds with rap artists, some of which were on his own record label. Even though Andre Harrell is the current president of Bad Boy Records, it is executive and mogul Sean Puffy Combs who is constantly making all of the gangster press as producer/artist. Others who took the spotlight from record executive to gangsta status include Russell Simmons of Def Jam Records fame and rapper Jay-Z (Shawn Carter), a.k.a Jigga Man, from Roc-A-Fella Records. You need not be a real gangster to achieve gangsta status.

Since N.W.A.'s smash record *Straight Outta Compton* hit the shelves, gangsta rap has been on the rise. Producer Dr. Dre's *Chronic* not only sold more records than any other gangsta rap CD, but also featured the work of upstart rapper Calvin Broadus, otherwise known as Snoop Doggy Dogg. Not many people know that Snoop was discovered by his cousin Warren G and Dr. Dre as a replacement for Ice Cube in N.W.A. After recording this record, Snoop Dogg scored big with hits from his *Next Episode* CD, and solo CDs *Dogg Pound* and *Doggfather* were produced by Dr. Dre.

Dr. Dre is the undisputed king of gangsta rap. Other artists that Dre produced include Eminem, Xzibit, and Nate Dogg. Nate Dogg is a vocalist who appears on many rappers' recordings because of his monotone rap-style singing. His smooth ghetto style sound is a desired *flava* on many recordings. Just listen to him singing on "Regulate" or Mista Grimm's "Indo Smoke"!

Dr. Dre

Some of the current gangsta rap artists include The Game, E-40, Kurupt, Murder Inc., Ice Cube, Daz, Wu-Tang Clan, DMX, Mystikal, and 50 Cent.

Hip-Hop Ambience

As was mentioned in the last chapter, this author believes Hip-Hop to have a sound that is loud, rude, and obnoxious. The bass rumbles woofers and can be heard in a *drop top 6/4 with the windows fogged* a mile away. The highs are piercing and could break glass. The ambience of Hip-Hop is extreme. We have examined some of Hip-Hop's combined elements such as hits, squeals, scratches, and gangsta groove. The next step is to get a handle on its overall **ambience**: what are those sounds that are non-musical, yet musical? What are those sounds that are dirty, muffled, and confusing? What is that racket?

Racket is a term that I have given to just that. It is the noisy effects on a recording that, at first listen, do not appear to sound musical. If the recording did not possess those sounds, they would be missed and, therefore, would not have the same sound effect. Because of this reason, Hip-Hop ambience or racket is musical.

On the R&B classic "Can't Get Next to You" by the Temptations, the song starts out with the sounds of friends gathered together about to have a party or maybe a drink. The sound or atmosphere created as a result was musical racket. Another example is the party atmosphere that was created on the beginning of Marvin Gaye's soul classic, "What's Going On?" In funk music, a bass guitar part can include slap, pluck, and pop sounds. When used as part of musical racket, these bass sounds take on a different character compared to how they might be used as part of a bass melody. In Hip-Hop, if a producer purposely samples the sound of a vinyl record pop sound, he/she is using racket for ambience.

Reverse samples can be used as racket, as well as explosions, ice cream truck bells, gunshot sounds, a woman's scream, and baby nuances, which are all used in Hip-Hop. It is important to note that producers don't just include this racket for the hell of it. They are attempting to add ambience and sonic environment so as to enhance the overall musical experience and deliver presence to the message of the song.

Another aspect of Hip-Hop ambience is **polytonality**: two or more different keys or tonalities being played at the same time. As stated earlier, Hip-Hop songwriters and producers use different colors or flava instead of traditional melodic and harmonic ideas. For example, a Hip-Hop song may contain a sample of a horn stab with one melody, and a vocal sample with a different melody, and the bass line in an entirely different key from the other instrumentation. This result, to an untrained ear, is good flava. To a musically trained ear it sounds crazy.

The interesting thing is that, although I have a trained musical ear and can understand traditional theoretics, I can also hear the symmetry within these types of arrangements. In other words, with careful listening, over time the ear will accept these types of harmonic and melodic inconsistencies. The result of polytonality in Hip-Hop is dissonance, and throughout musical history, dissonance has always been relative. Over time it becomes accepted and invaluable.

The Vocoder Effect

A **vocoder** is a keyboard instrument that, combined with a vocal effects processor and microphone, produces robotic-like vocal sounds when played simultaneously with singing. The vocoder can also be an external rack mount effect compatible with other electronic instruments. It has a similar sound and function as the *tube* effect known as the *talk box.* Nowadays, vocoders come built into workstation keyboards as hybrid hardware effects, or are included in software packages with virtual instruments. The vocoder was originally made popular in early 1980s Euro techno pop, but soon found its way into R&B, funk, and Hip-Hop.

R&B and funk songs that popularized the talk box include Rufus's "Tell Me Something Good," Zapp/Roger Troutman's "More Bounce to the Ounce," and Midnight Star's "Freak-A-Zoid." Other R&B and funk vocoder pioneers included Earth, Wind & Fire with "Let's Groove," Herbie Hancock's "Rock It," and One Way's "Mr. Groove."

In early Hip-Hop, Afrika Bambaataa's groups Zulu Nation and Soul Sonic Force both used vocoder frequently on dance tracks. Other Hip-Hop artists/songs known for the use of vocoders as ambience were Kano's "I'm Ready," Houdini's "5 Minutes of Funk," Ollie Brown & Jerry Knight's "Electric Boogaloo," "California Love" by Tupac, "Cali Iz Active" by Snoop Dogg & Dogg Pound featuring Ice Cube (which also uses a heavy backbeat push feel or *metric displacement,* see Chapter 9, p. 70), and Grandmaster Flash's "Scorpio (Show No Shame)."

The following examples exhibit various gangsta grooves. They include lots of racket and ambience. Be sure to play the parts with the same feel that the groove dictates. Try to identify all of the racket that you hear, and simulate it on your keyboard during the play-along track.

So Just Chill

TRACK 46

Get Yo Money

TRACK 47

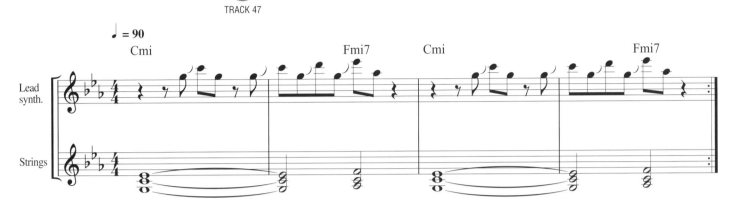

Gangsta Karma

TRACK 48

Family Ties

TRACK 49

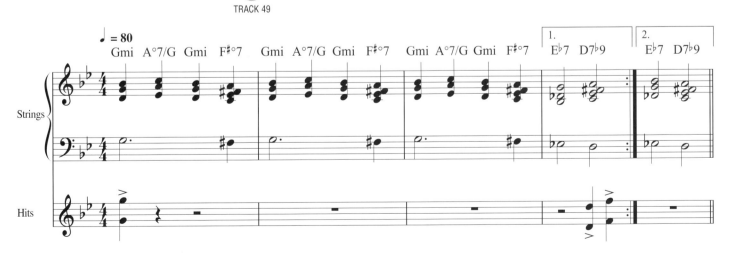

A G Rollin' Up

TRACK 50

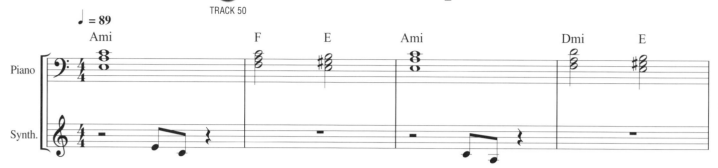

Sit on the Wall

TRACK 51

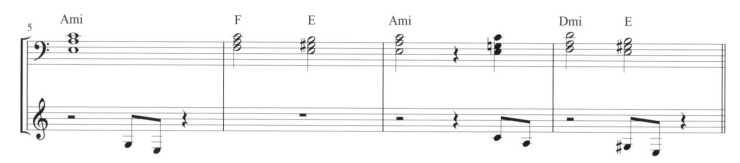

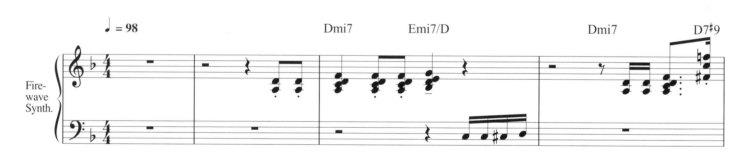

What U Workin'

TRACK 52

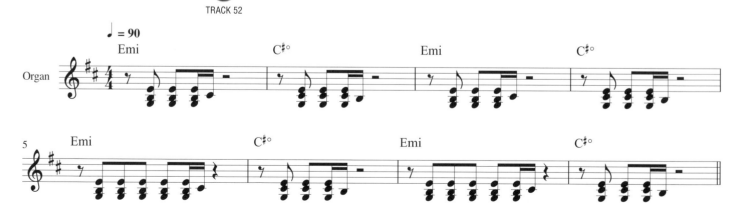

N Da Club Mix

TRACK 53

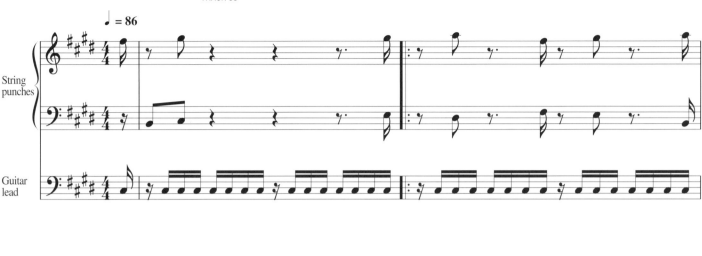

Chapter Eight

8 SEQUENCING, SOUND LIBRARIES, AND STUFF

This chapter will focus on Hip-Hop songwriters and artists preparing for the twenty-first century by becoming producers. With so many technological breakthroughs for creating and recording music available to artists, the need for an outside producer is becoming less and less necessary. In the contemporary styles of rap and Hip-Hop, the rappers and singers have rapidly become quite skilled at sampling, recording, and songwriting at home. What has become the icing on the cake is the ability to produce high quality demos, which is now the industry standard. No longer will A&R accept poorly recorded and produced songs.

Presently there is no need to pay outrageous production fees and recording studio fees only to have your songs sound like somebody else's song. You can become a self-contained keyboardist/ producer with your own recording studio. There are more opportunities for the Hip-Hop producer than for the artists. Keyboard players who are capable of becoming producers in this style are the liaisons between the artists and the record companies, and by extension, in line to score a record deal.

This chapter will also serve to inform you (the keyboard player) as to the possibilities in the expanding world of music production. As we progress into the new millennium, contemporary black music will focus more on melody, rhythm, harmony, and musicianship. Original music for rap, spoken word, recreations, new songs, film, and television will come back strong. The same rappers and singers who are getting high-profile gigs now will be unqualified to play music and create original songs. Now is the time for keyboard players to obtain the necessary skills to become good music producers. Learning how to sequence could be a fresh start towards a journey that will change your musical life.

Sequencing

The craft of **sequencing** (recording multiple tracks via MIDI) is becoming almost essential for Hip-Hop. There are many times in live scenarios when an artist requires a keyboard player to program complex introductions or arrange lavish strings or horns—parts that would be difficult or even impossible to actually perform live. The part may have too many changes, use too many different sounds, or last too long to sample it. When this occurs, a professional Hip-Hop keyboard player will sequence the pattern on his/her computer or workstation keyboard. When the sequence is committed to data, it can be called up and flawlessly performed within seconds. This is why we see many keyboard players onstage with computers. In this ever-changing music scene we are called upon more and more to do the impossible. While you are struggling to figure out how to play these types of patterns, someone else has been hired to do just what I have described.

This book will not teach you everything about how to sequence, but should give you a strong point of departure so that you will take the necessary steps towards gaining this skill. Brief liberty was taken in describing this process in Chapter 6. If the information here is a little more complicated, refer to the earlier chapter and review.

An introduction to sequencing Hip-Hop or any style starts with a basic objective, which is to learn the basics of navigating through sequencing software and learning workstation functions. You should learn the basics of recording, editing, and mixing musical passages and projects. You should also learn the processes of saving, loading, and transferring files to and from various media.

Learning sequencing includes working within a MIDI workstation environment, such as a setup including the Steinberg Cubase VST software, or perhaps a Macintosh system with Logic, Pro Tools, or even Garage Band.

The first step is to learn how to power up your gear, operate all of your equipment, and your system's log on/off procedures. You should give yourself a complete overview of the various screens or windows on your system, and also find out from an expert whether you have all of the equipment you need, including accessories and adapters.

You must learn real-time sequencing, how to set up and use the head phones and mixer, program drum sounds, operate transport bars and function buttons, and understand macro editors. You must also learn formatting and saving procedures in order to back up your files. In addition, functions such as copying/pasting procedures, your system's pull-down menus, toolbox, shortcuts (key-stroke commands), and selecting sounds should be familiarized. With computers or workstations, the undo/deleting, moving parts, and edit windows will be crucial to effectively sequence. You also may find it useful to learn about your score or notation function if you have one in your system.

Many times you will find it easier or more useful to employ step-record functions. If you are using a computer to sequence, then virtual instruments will undoubtedly be a part of your system specifications. You must learn the craft of creating sections of parts, and doing so using more than one instrument at a time, which is called **multi-tracking**.

You may find it useful with a computer system to arrange tracks with **coded organization**. The use of color-coded parts is helpful in identifying sections. If you are using a workstation keyboard, you will want to efficiently name sections, parts, etc. For example, "Intro/verse/chorus" should be clearly mapped, as well as your instruments' classifications and locations, which should also be organized. Using custom arranges (templates designed for the user to select functions, parameters, and visual layout) and notepad programs can help keep things organized as well. You must also be able to import SMFs (Standard MIDI Files). Having control over your data will make life much simpler for you, whether you're sequencing for live performance or the studio.

Libraries and Stuff

The Hip-Hop keyboard player who is making the transformation to producer must have a strong handle on the latest technology. He/she must obtain the latest software and have unlimited access to sample libraries. The factory library of sounds for your workstation is a standard library that would be to your benefit to have in your possession. What about the song files you have created? All back-up files for SYS-EX system exclusive files would be nice to have as well, in addition to virtual instrument files, software update files, notation files, audio wave files, and i-Tunes files.

If you have the persistence and know-how in this genre, you could become a Foley person, film composer, television musical director, music supervisor on Hip-Hop film projects, production coordinator for a recording studio, or even a major producer. It all starts right where you are at right now. It requires the ability to stay informed and the passion to stay on top of your game as a musician and producer. As a producer, think of your information, data, and song files as money, and the libraries as banks for your money. The more you save, the wealthier you are!

The flow of information is endless, and the need to keep all the information intact is imperative in the routine maintenance of a library. The key to staying on top of this endless resource of information is to organize these files into libraries. Many of the libraries mentioned are available on the market, and in some cases, the means by which to organize itself are built in. If this is the case, then that makes it simple to achieve. Sometime you, as the keyboard player/producer, must do the organizing and updating yourself. In the old days, we used floppy disks and external storage devices to handle the excess data. Nowadays, you can store nearly all of your data on CDs or DVDs.

In Hip-Hop, the sample is the building block of song creation. It would be a good idea to begin with the systematic storage of all your samples. Once you have them categorized alphabetically you should put them into some sort of order by sound. I actually have a sound-effect CD library that includes some samples I have created, and are stored separately. That way if I ever need just a group of sounds that are similar to the ones I have created, I don't have to search all over the place for a certain kind of sampled sound. As producer you are free to choose any type of organization you like, but as they say in the studio, "time is money," so don't waste your time.

The idea is to keep your system well equipped to handle any task that you may be called upon to execute. Your ultimate goal as keyboard player/producer is to get the job done right. Most of all, remember that technology is only a tool for your creativity. Once you let it make the decisions for you, you become a carpenter being hit on the head by his own hammer. Stay in control! These keyboards are only machines—don't let them dictate what you can or cannot do.

Survive and Tour Until Fame and Fortune: S.T.U.F.F.

I'm sure you've heard of the phrases "fake it till you make it" and "get in where you fit in." Well, that's kind of the message here about being successful as a keyboard player in Hip-Hop. There are no guarantees of success, only of failure, if you don't try. As a player, my rule of thumb has always been to survive. It does not make sense to exploit your talents and skills as a keyboard player if it does not benefit you financially. You can play for exposure and experience, but at some point you have to survive, even if it means taking some other kind of non-musical job. It could aid in financing your dream of musical success.

Performing on the road with a working artist is a good option for any musician. It requires you to be talented, professional, adaptable, and easy to get along with. Doing so will teach you a lot about the entertainment business. Even the audition process can be a useful experience. The main thing it can do is get you paid and exposed out on a high level in the music industry. It also serves to get you valuable experience that can transfer to just about any facet of the music business, as long as you can observe and absorb the right information. You must, however, see the light at the end of the tunnel and know when that type of work has run its course.

Fame and fortune are relative. You don't want to be famous for doing something stupid, or have great fortune only to lose it by doing something. In other words, you've got to be smart going after what you want. You must stop, look, and listen! You've got to be aware of your plans, hopes, and dreams, and be able to set an effective course of action. In order to handle being famous or having great wealth, you must be mentally and spiritually ready for it. Having said all that, I prefer having the fame and fortune! Just be careful for what you wish for, because it may come true. The world of Hip-Hop is wide open for new artists, new ideas, and new keyboard players, so go for it!

The following examples contain elements of Hip-Hop patterns that utilize the possibilities of integrating sequences and sample libraries into recordings. Many of the sounds demonstrated here as arrangements and orchestrations are commonly used throughout the Hip-Hop music of today.

In "Butta," the track starts with a vinyl scratch sound that can be found on many stereo effects racks and sample libraries. Listen to how it sets up the ambience and enhances the Rhodes part that is being played with metric displacement. Most of the orchestration has been eliminated in the play-along version of the track so you can find the placement of the Rhodes part with the drums. This is the kind of arrangement found in neo-soul as well.

Butta

TRACK 54

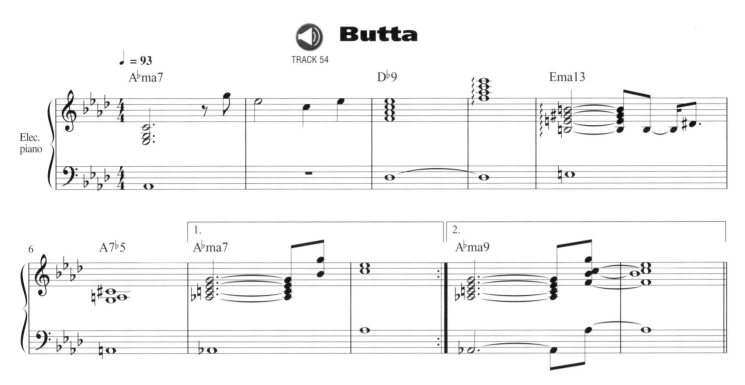

The starkness of the track "Powder" allows for the space of the rhythm to be heard better. The Rhodes part has a slight swing feel in order to have it sit better with the drum track, which is also using metric displacement (see Chapter 9, p. 70). This type of sequenced feel is common when recording tracks to an Akai MPC.

Powder

TRACK 55

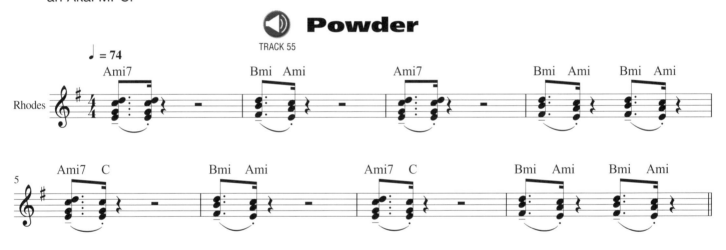

In "Gold & Silver," the phrasing of the lead synthesizer employs dynamics and accents. Be sure to phrase tightly and lock in with the drums. Keep in mind that the drum part is a common type of sequenced feel heard in Hip-Hop.

Gold & Silver

TRACK 56

In "Iced Up," the parts are multi-layered. Although they are not difficult to play, the execution of the rhythm has to achieve an almost quantized-like feel in order to match the inhuman drum and bass parts often created in Hip-Hop sequences.

Iced Up

TRACK 57

"You Buggin' " has multi-layered melody lines which create an almost confusing syncopated effect. The lead synthesizer line is designed to bounce against the orchestra hits, strings line, and bass line. This kind of chaotic sequence pattern can be heard in Hip-Hop tracks by artists like E-40, Jay-Z, Dr. Dre, Nelly, and many others.

You Buggin'

TRACK 58

In the next example, "Wicked Girls," the Phrygian/harmonic minor melody, syncopated kick drum rhythm, and vibrato lead synthesizer effect make this pattern interesting to play. The challenge is to lock your part up and keep it grooving throughout the entire exercise. Listen carefully to the play-along version on the track. The wah guitar sound is a sample. Can you hear the wicked girl laugh? This subtle sound came from the author's sample library.

 **Wicked Girls**

TRACK 59

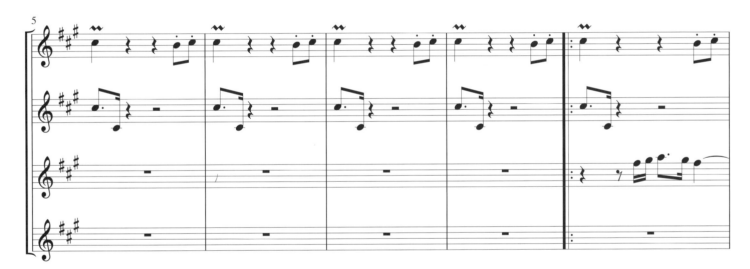

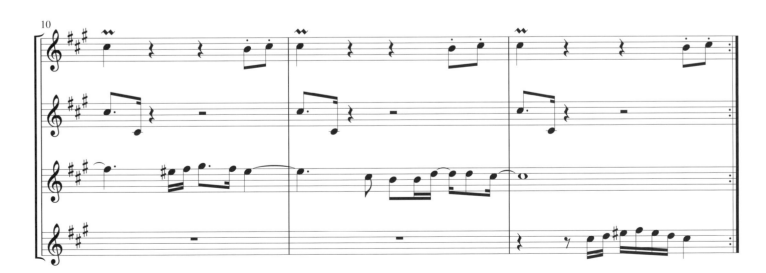

"Gotta Bounce" uses a polyphonic synthesizer, which must be played with a heavy swing feel. Be patient with the phrasing so that your part sits way back in the groove. Also listen to the sample of vocal snippets and percussion sounds that have a pitch bend effect.

Gotta Bounce

TRACK 60

In "Snake Charmer," the lead synthesizer line uses another harmonic minor/Arabic modal melody to give this track a Middle-Eastern sound. Many Hip-Hop artists like Nelly, Sunshine Anderson, and Kanye West are beginning to use this type of melody. Listen to the samples of vocal snippets and vocoder effects which are used very often in Hip-Hop tracks. The gong, tabla, and buzzed snare drums are all samples.

Snake Charmer

TRACK 61

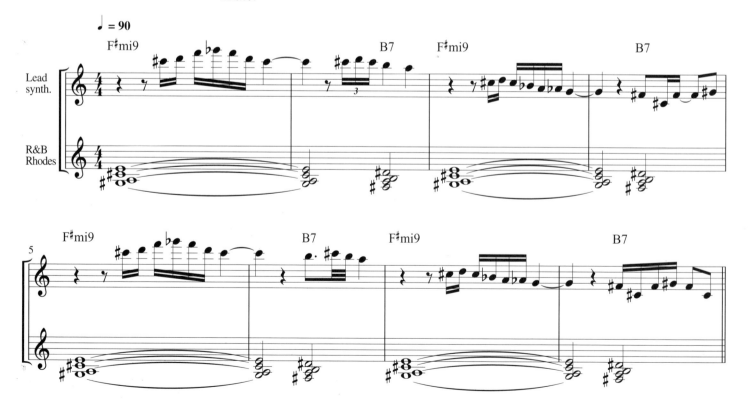

Chapter Nine

9 PLAYING DJ, PLAYING LIVE, AND PLAYING TRACKS

ip-Hop is presently evolving into a genre with its own set of rules, its own distinct characteristics, and is changing the landscape of musical orchestration. It is quite common in today's Hip-Hop world to see a string section with a DJ live on stage. It is equally common to hear a jazz trio with electronic synthesizer and studio-generated effects on a Hip-Hop record. Another common orchestral practice is to mix and match instruments from one genre to another in studio demos and project recordings, including mixing in some home songwriter recording ideas. In other words, many of the rules formerly adhered to are being routinely and systematically broken. Experimentation of orchestration and arrangement ideas is encouraged, with one exception. It is strongly recommended that before you break the rules, you take the time, training, and effort to first learn them. For example, if you are composing a Hip-Hop song with a feel and sound from the 1980s, then you wouldn't put an acoustic bass or strings in your arrangements. On the other hand, if you are borrowing feel or sounds from that period of time, but your composition is structured from the present rules of Hip-Hop, then it would make sense to make that kind of an abstract choice. It is a subtle difference, but nevertheless, one that should be taken under consideration.

In the midst of all of this change and upheaval is you, the keyboard player. Keyboard players are now expected to emulate the DJ's role in Hip-Hop music. Since DJ-type sounds have been included on modern keyboards and synthesizers, you are now being expected to not only play your keyboard parts, but the DJ's parts as well. Many artists and bands either cannot afford, or choose not to pay for a DJ. Since keyboard players are ordinarily hired as utility players within the rhythm section, taking on this chore is a feasible option.

Playing DJ

The disc jockey had a huge role in the musical creation and ultimate evolution of Hip-Hop. Without going into complete detail, suffice it to say that understanding the contributions of the DJ warrants study. You must observe the way a DJ historically mixed sounds, hooks, licks, and especially hits. The DJ always had a keen sense of the needs of the audience. In carefully watching their movements, noticing their reaction to certain patterns and rhythms became one of the DJ's fortes.

One of the greatest DJs was the infamous Grandmaster Flash. Flash (Joseph Saddler), originally from Barbados, started his career in 1976 under the tutelage of the great DJ Herc. Flash and Kid Creole (known widely for his group Kid Creole & the Coconuts) later formed the Furious Five who signed with Sugarhill Records (Sylvia Robinson's label) and made Hip-Hop history. Grandmaster Flash went on to become one of the world's greatest DJs. Many credit Flash for the creation of the scratch technique!

Since Flash was there at the start of it all, he had to interact with musicians and producers. In order to be effective, you must interact with DJs. Today there are thousands of budding DJs looking for performing experience. You should team up with some of these musicians and exchange information and ideas. Gaining this experience will put a nice lid on your DJ abilities and provide you with valuable insight into the world of Hip-Hop.

The DJ was master of hype and kept the crowd entertained. You may not want to be the front man in your act while playing live, but you must accept the front man mentality in order to play your DJ keyboard parts effectively. Be sure to turn your effects up loud enough to be heard when you are performing, and remember, play with lots of dynamics!

Playing Live

Traditionally, keyboard players playing with Hip-Hop artists were R&B or funk players. Since the DJ was king in this style of music, the keyboard player did not receive a lot of props. What most of these players did was comp existing parts from old records. Doing this live wasn't very creative, and in fact it wasn't different from playing an R&B song in a cover band. It did, however, take a person with a good ear and good understanding of the works of other keyboard players like Bernie Worrell of Parliament; Larry Dunn of Earth, Wind & Fire; or Billie Beck of the Ohio Players. R&B keyboard players laid the foundation for Hip-Hop. It is recommended that you listen to the works of these and many other players from that era. If you study my *R&B Soul Keyboards* book, you will see a comprehensive list of several keyboardists and songs to study.

The earliest known Hip-Hop band was Stetsasonic. This Brooklyn, NY-based group formed in 1981 and scored marginal hit CDs. Stetsasonic members and producers Prince Paul and Daddy-O became more successful as producers for Hip-Hop artists De La Soul, Mary J. Blige, and Red Hot Chili Peppers. One of the best live Hip-Hop bands was the Roots. This group was formed in Philadelphia, Pennsylvania in 1992. They modeled themselves after Stetsasonic. The Roots' keyboard player Scott Storch and MC Black Thought were instrumental in their development, and set into motion a whole new way of performing Hip-Hop music. Storch later retired from playing with the group, but continued to write parts for new keyboardist, Kamal Gray. Some of the CDs made famous by the Roots were *Organix* (live debut), *Illadelph Halflife*, and *Things Fall Apart*. Some of the artists that the Roots performed with included Nas, Talib Kweli, Big Daddy Kane, Erykah Badu, Common, D'Angelo, Jay-Z and Mos Def. They were known for their unusual *sample-free* Hip-Hop music CDs. Their work should be studied.

Photo: Haley Madden, Redferns Music Picture Library

Roots

Most keyboard players currently playing live with Hip-Hop acts are talented but unknown. The keyboard player must now possess skills beyond that of the older players, yet maintain a feel and sensibility of modern music. Hip-Hop artists find that black gospel players have those skills. They have great ears, outstanding feel, superb technique, and foremost, they fully understand modern music. Gospel players are capable of routinely improvising new exploratory keyboard parts while maintaining the song's essence and thrust.

Most gospel keyboard players learned music on pianos or modern synthesizers right in the churches. Many of them were part of musical ministry programs. This added benefit made them ideal candidates for performing with Hip-Hop artists. In most cases these keyboardists did not read or write music, but that is not a prerequisite for Hip-Hop. If you don't have that kind of musical background, it does not prohibit you from getting this type of work, but it would be a great idea to study gospel keyboards as well. As a start, one may try the keyboard instruction book *Gospel Piano*, published by Hal Leonard Corporation.

The Metric Displacement Phenomenon

In Hip-Hop, rhythm, feel, and groove are key components to the style. Much of this is a result of musicians coming up with ideas while playing live music. Playing live within the Hip-Hop genre involves several aspects. The first aspect is to understand the different feels or grooves. The most common feel of a Hip-Hop keyboard part is to play with a slight delay or hesitation to the rhythmic placements of the beat. This kind of feel is called *laid back* or playing *behind the groove*. Although playing behind the groove was done often in R&B, it is even more exaggerated in Hip-Hop. In this book, we will refer to this rhythmic phenomenon as **metric displacement**.

A good example of this occurs in the composition performed by Michael Jackson called "Butterflies." The drum pattern and the keyboard parts both have a laid-back feel. Listen to determine if you can hear this unique metric displacement of the rhythm. It takes a good deal of time and effort to find the exact placement of this feel, but some time spent with a drum machine or good drummer should speed up the process.

Nowadays, the displacement is occurring on an anticipated beat 2 of a common Hip-Hop back beat. This type of rushed feel on a single beat is called *push feel*. This anticipation or push feel was common in R&B, but the difference is that in Hip-Hop, the feel of the groove stays laid back while the push occurs within each bar at the exact same place. Wow! Check out this chart that describes various feels.

How It Feels Throughout of the Eras of African American Music

African American keyboard music can be described in six basic aspects of feel. They are as follows:

1. Loose and laid back ('50s Doo Wop, '60s Stax, '70s soul)

2. Tight and on top ('50s gospel, '60s Brown, '80s Prince, '70s funk)

3. Syncopated & aggressive, but laid back ('50s jump blues, '60s Sly, '90s Hip-Hop)

4. Tight and smooth ('60s Motown, '70s Philly soul)

5. Loose but aggressive ('60s rock, '70s P-funk, '90s rap)

6. Heavy syncopation with *metric displacement* (Y2K–present Hip-Hop)

Making a Sound Choice

Another aspect of live playing is using the right sounds. This goes without saying for almost every other genre as well, but it bears a unique quality for Hip-Hop. For example, acoustic piano sounds for Hip-Hop have a very cutting quality to them. Just as an old upright honky-tonk is great for blues, you must find just the right sharpness of tone for Hip-Hop. The parts played are usually very simple but have a powerful attack and presence. The electric piano sounds are very warm and rich, and usually consist of either Fender Rhodes or Wurlitzer piano sounds. This choice of sound is borrowed from the R&B soul sounds of the 1970s, but still possess a unique Y2K sensibility, particularly the keyboard **voicings** (how notes are spaced within a chord for color and voice leading). Equally important is the articulation or the approach to striking the keys, to the end result of establishing authenticity. Some keyboard sampler or synthesizer sounds are such a huge part of the song that if they were not present in the live show, the performance would be lacking.

Hip-Hop artists are relying heavily on their keyboard players to recreate the textural environment they established on their recordings. It is imperative to use the right samples, sounds, and colors in order to remain current and viable as a keyboard player.

The third and most compelling aspect to playing Hip-Hop live is the ability to improvise. It used to be commonplace in rap and Hip-Hop for keyboard players to stick to playing only the parts that were played on the original recordings. Nowadays, the artists usually want the parts to be played accurately, but with even more feel, rhythm, and groove—with more flava! In other words, they want the keyboard parts hyped as well.

What this translates to the keyboard player to do is to add a little something extra to the chords, melodies, rhythms, and the overall tonality or sound of the parts. This liberty of changing color should add a fresh new approach to what you will play live. In essence, you are expected to create a remixed or new arrangement of your part.

This is becoming more and more prevalent in the world of live Hip-Hop. It is also challenging without some kind of formal instruction or understanding of improvisation. For all of these elements mentioned, there is a viable solution. Some instruction in music theory, particularly jazz theory, is recommended. In studying jazz, you can find many new ways of experimenting with these aspects, and even develop a good method for improvisation. This will certainly aid in your ability to create a new vibe for your parts. Again, adhere to the main structure and character of the Hip-Hop style when integrating these other methods and ideas.

Playing Tracks

Nowadays, the keyboard player is expected to sequence tracks, play the keyboard track live, and synchronize the pre-recorded studio tracks or trigger samples of them onstage (perhaps via computer). In order to do this, a Hip-Hop keyboard player must know how to get the best results in any of these scenarios, especially since the role of keyboardist is ever changing. The least daunting of the tasks is the duty of sequencing. Nearly all the workstations sold on the present market have sequencing capability, and the instruction information is obtainable.

Keyboard players should always be able to play in a rhythm section, and should equally be comfortable playing with recorded tracks. In Hip-Hop, the keyboard player is usually the one who is up until 3:00 a.m. cutting the tracks being played. Even though this fact is a given, it may be awkward performing live. It is certainly much different than playing with an actual drummer and bass player.

In a live situation, you must be able to put on headphones or an ear piece and sync up your feel with a computer, MPC, or workstation keyboard sequencer. You must stay focused, wear several musical hats, and still be aware of what is going on onstage and in your audience. For a professional Hip-Hop keyboard player, these activities are nothing more than another day at the office.

The technical aspects of tracking and triggering (and/or sampling) via computer may be learned by studying musical electronics, or by taking recording classes. This will take some time and persistence, but the end result will be a flourishing career in Hip-Hop and beyond. The opportunities for a skilled electronic musical arranger/technician are abundant and highly lucrative. If you are leaning toward this side of the Hip-Hop keyboard world, consider studying with an expert or take formal classes at a school.

Being able to create tracks could help you to work closely with songwriters, artists, and producers. At any rate, playing keyboard tracks should be a key point on your musical resume. By observing and effectively executing all of the exercises, nuances, and points presented in each chapter of this book, you are now ready to excel in the ranks of the Contemporary Hip-Hop Keyboard Player!

The following examples are presented to demonstrate the different characteristics and aspects of playing keyboards within each afore-described scenario. The exercises contain patterns found in all of the most common types of classic Hip-Hop songs. These patterns will focus heavily on L.H. and R.H. independence. Again, try to establish the right sounds and sample effects on your keyboard in order to play these exercises. Listen carefully to the placement of these parts, particularly the differences between live and tracks. Last, but not least, make sure you are wearing the right hat for each of these examples. Ask yourself the right questions. Are you playing the DJ's role? Is this a live feel or am I sticking to the book with tracks? As usual, playing example tracks are provided for you to play along with the CD. Most of all, have fun and make it groove!

Fill Me In Later

TRACK 62

Scorchin'

TRACK 63

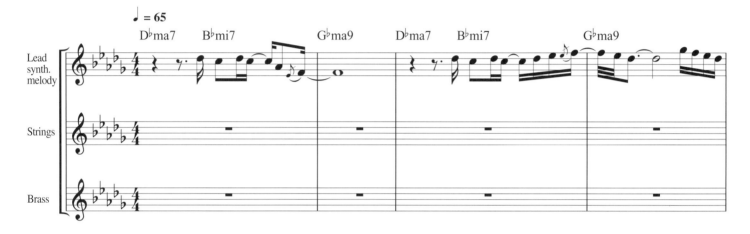

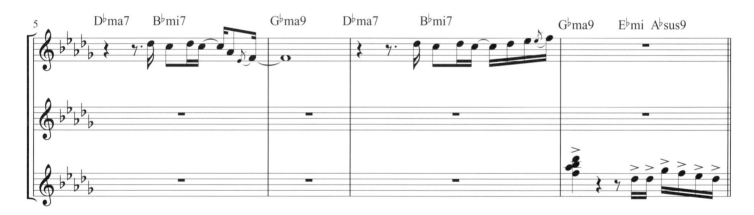

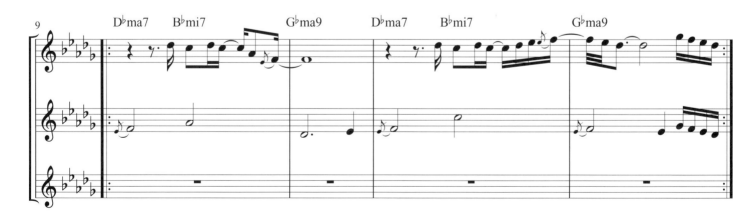

Pushing Me

TRACK 64

Here 2 Stay

TRACK 65

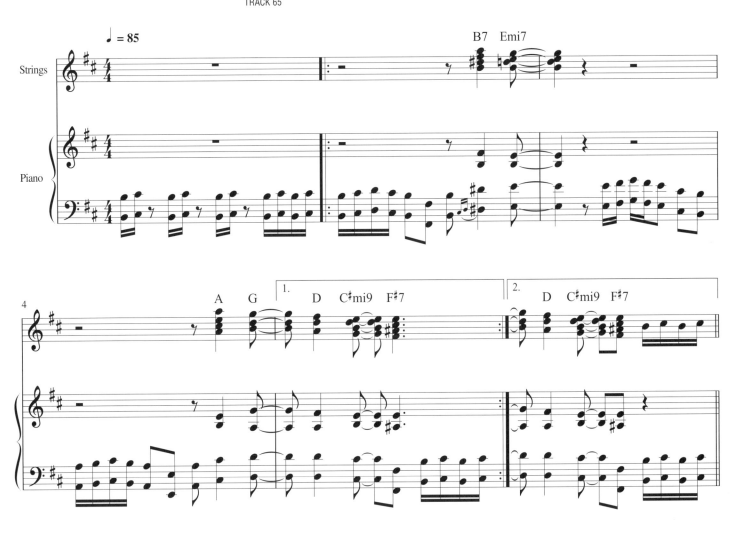

Connie's Good-bye

TRACK 66

Dope Lope

TRACK 67

Ballad Wishes

TRACK 68

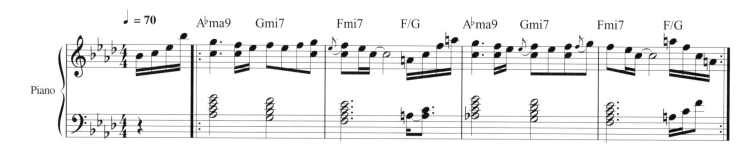

Gone Fishing

TRACK 69

Chapter Ten

10 THE CONTEMPORARY HIP-HOP KEYBOARDIST

The role of the keyboard player is ever-changing in the style of Hip-Hop. As stated in earlier chapters, a keyboard player must be able to play existing parts accurately and with authority. They need to understand the fundamentals of groove, and be able to handle syncopated lead lines and chord rhythms. A keyboardist must also be proficient at creating and playing good solid bass lines. Additionally, a keyboard player should be able to simulate DJ scratches/effects, and set up various structural sections within the song by playing hits, squeals, and related racket. Keyboard players should also know the fundamentals of the studio as well as have a good understanding of sequencing and sampling for live or demo projects. This is the overall duty of the contemporary Hip-Hop keyboardist. Even though this is a myriad of assignments and possibilities, the greatest challenge could be in fully understanding the purpose and structure of the style itself. A contemporary Hip-Hop keyboard player must know the proper sounds, historic direction, and especially the future thrust of Hip-Hop!

Few can argue that Hip-Hop is evolving into many brands and sub-genres. The key to understanding this fully lies in the rhythm. Hip-Hop rhythms have always been funky, syncopated, and over-flowing with attitude. There are quite a few rhythmic structures and expressions to observe in order to fully intuit the next direction of Hip-Hop music. It takes an *ear to the beat* of the street to anticipate its next move. The contemporary Hip-Hop keyboardist is one who not only can play the existing style with confidence, but also can catch the wave of the coming groove. Let's examine the modern movement.

Hip-Hop and Rap Rock

From the early days of rap, there has been a movement to unite the worlds of Hip-Hop and rock. Such unifications include Run-DMC's teaming up with Aerosmith on their remake of "Walk This Way," Snoop Dogg's touring collaboration with Linkin Park and Korn, the Beastie Boys, Kid Rock, Ice-T's rock band Body Count, and many more. The contemporary Hip-Hop keyboardist should have a handle on the characteristics of this sub-genre which is soon to become a full-blown musical style!

Rap Soap Operas

As explained in Chapter 1 in the "Parody and Novelty Rap" section, comedic stories and song ideas have gained popularity and have been responsible for many hits within the Hip-Hop culture. Even the Remix Producers used rhymes and humorous story lines to propel their sampled tunes into the consciousness of their listeners, as further explained in the same chapter.

A current trend and somewhat related idea is to produce music with dramatic and continued story lines. The thrust of this movement has been to do so with a healthy dose of comedy within the rap and melodies of each lyric. Leading the charge of this Rap Soap Opera genre is the multi-talented and controversial artist R. Kelly.

R. Kelly (Robert Sylvester Kelly) came on the scene in the early 1990s as lead singer of Public Announcement. Shortly thereafter he became known for many hit songs, including "I Believe I Can Fly," "Bump N' Grind," "Step in the Name of Love," and many more. His songwriting skills led him to mega-hit collaborations with some of Hip-Hop's giants, such as "Down Low" with Ron Isley & the Isley Brothers, "Home Alone" with Keith Murray, "That's that Sh*t" with Snoop Dogg, and other songs, including Michael Jackson's "From the Bottom of My Heart" and Usher's "Same Girl."

The song "Contagious," featuring Ron Isley & Chante Moore, along with "Showdown," a follow-up, can be looked upon as Rap Soap Opera because each song is lyrically connected to each other's story line.

Kelly's unique way of creating explicit and candid lyrics that rhyme perfectly into his rapid-fire story lines led him to writing the poetically brilliant "Trapped in the Closet, Chapters 1–5." This ingenious Rap Soap Opera must be heard to be believed. In tradition, his cliff-hanger endings leave you wanting more. This new genre must be studied more thoroughly, and must be viewed as a new wave in Hip-Hop. By extension, the content and structure must be understood by the contemporary Hip-Hop keyboardist.

The Evolution of Polyrhythm

Polyrhythm is the use of one or more meters being played simultaneously and in sync with each other. It can be patterns of three in groups of four, or patterns of two in groups of three, etc. Polyrhythm is by no means a new phenomenon. It originated in many of the cultures of ancient Africa. It can be heard in the native drum patterns of Ethiopia, Nigeria, the Congo, West Africa, Azania, Egypt, and the West Indies. Polyrhythm ventured worldwide and has traveled into Asia, Europe, Cuba, Peru, the Islands, the Americas, and just about everywhere. It has made a resurgence in African American styles such as jazz, reggae, R&B, funk, and fusion. It is present in all Afro-Cuban, Timba, Caribbean Soca, Brazilian, and Salsa music. These styles are very popular worldwide, but have not been as popular here in the U.S. Although the influence of polyrhythm is felt here in America, this chapter will draw parallels from its R&B source.

Polyrhythmic patterns can be heard in the song "Serpentine Fire" by Earth, Wind & Fire. The drums play in 4/4, the horns play double time, and the guitar and keyboards play even faster. The Ohio Players' "Love Rollercoaster" includes a breakdown section where the rhythm guitar plays in 4/4 while the drum plays a half-time feel, out of sync—very clever. Soul artist Donny Hathaway's song "This Christmas" includes a great 7/4 hook that can be played as 4/4 or any other variation of groups of four.

Hip-Hop is beginning to use more and more polyrhythm within its song form. An example of polyrhythm in a Hip-Hop song is Eminem's "Forgot About Dre." The rhythm has a half-time feel, while Eminem raps with a double-time feel. The result is an effective multidimensional rhythmic groove.

The Timbaland Influence

One Hip-Hop musician/producer who is well-known for his use of stagnant and syncopated polyrhythms is Timbaland. Timothy Timbaland Mosley started his career as a rapper with his group Timbaland & Magoo in 1995. His use of heavy stuttered syncopated beats and effective bass patterns made him a leader in the current world of Hip-Hop. His unique use of heavy accents, crispy hi-hats, innovative squeals, and samples has elevated him to the top of the game as a producer. His alliance with childhood friend Missy Elliott led him to million dollar production work for artists like (the late) Aaliyah, Jay-Z, Justin Timberlake, Ginuwine, Tweet, the Game, Nelly Furtado, and Ludacris. All Hip-Hop artists are familiar with the sound, feel, and overwhelming influence of Timbaland on the genre.

Timbaland

Dirty South, Southern Rap, and Crunk

Timbaland is a native of Virginia, who, along with regional rappers from Tennessee, South Carolina, Florida, Georgia, and Louisiana, has formed a coalition of successful southern artists known as *Dirty South*. This alliance of regional Hip-Hop has given the East Coast and West Coast a run for its money, and, since the early 1990s, has firmly established the *Dirty South Coast* as an entity in Hip-Hop! Other Dirty South artists include Luther Campbell, OutKast, Master P, Lil' Wayne, Lil' Romeo, Juvenile, Mystikal, Missy Elliott, D-Jay, Gangsta Boo, E-40, Lil' Jon, Ludacris, Mase, T-Pain, Arrested Development, and dozens of others. *Southern rap* and *Crunk* are even deeper sub-genres of the Dirty South influence.

Mainstream Hip-Hop Artists

Today, Hip-Hop has reached mainstream status. Many of its artists are so well-known that they may be considered household names. Some of these artists include Nelly, Usher, Mary J. Blige, Missy Elliott, Ice Cube, Snoop Dogg, OutKast, and Queen Latifah.

Reggae's Influence

Reggae is a style developed in Jamaica during the late 1940s and early 1950s. It consists of heavy rhythmic backbeats, colorful harmonies, and warm, rich melodies. It uses island rhythms, African sounds, African American groove concepts, and a soulful, unique, laid-back vocal style as an anchor for its powerful, lyrical messages of love, hope, and socio-political values. Artists like Bob Marley, Jimmy Cliff, and Third World are world renowned. Reggae is rooted in spiritual and ancestral reverence, and is derived from the Rastafarian faith. Reggae has always been a tremendous influence on all African American music, and Hip-Hop is no exception. Hip-Hop artists like the Roots, the Fugees, Wyclef Jean, Shabba Ranks, and Jah Rule have clear reggae influence.

Ska, Dancehall, and Reggaeton

Ska is a Jamaican style of music originating in the 1930s. It holds a mixture of Calypso and African American jazz influences. The sounds, arrangements, and orchestration have been an influence on Hip-Hop worldwide. It is recommended that you listen to ska and try to notice its connection to reggae.

Dancehall is a derivative of reggae started in Jamaica that has more emphasis on up-tempo beats. Like Hip-Hop, its origins include experimental innovations from the DJs or *Raggamuffins*, and incorporate dance influenced rhythms with *preach-style* rap. Two well-known Dancehall artists are Sean Paul, who recorded "Temperature," and Shaggy, who performed the hit song "It Wasn't Me."

Reggaeton is a derivative style that originated in Panama during the early 1990s. It is a combination of reggae and Hip-Hop. It uses heavy Hip-Hop rhythms along with the sounds and environment normally associated with reggae. It also has strong vocal rhythms and raps. Reggaeton performers center around the DJ or MC influence, and hype. Even though it is mainly heard in the Puerto Rican culture, it is becoming accepted in nearly all Spanish-speaking cultures, including the U.S. It is most likely the next phase of Hip-Hop's rhythmic development, and is becoming widely popular among African Americans and Anglo Americans. Some artists known for this style include Pitbull, Bobby Dixon, Shabba Ranks (Dem Bow), and Daddy Yankee.

The Neo-Soul Movement

During the mid 1990s, some Hip-Hop artists began to turn to their soul music roots and started experimenting with a cross mix of jazz, Hip-Hop, and ole school soul music. Neo soul has become a cross sector of Hip-Hop and now enjoys both older and younger music audiences. Artists like Soul II Soul, Brand New Heavies, Sound of Blackness, Lauryn Hill, and many others pioneered the way, and now look to the budding neo-soul sound for creativity. This movement led the way for artists like Erykah Badu, Jill Scott, Raphael Saadiq, Desi'ree, Mike Phillips, Amel Larrieux, Floetry, Anthony Hamilton, Alicia Keys, Leela James, Frank McComb, and Kem, who are all sharing much success in the neo-soul genre. Many of these artists share the same company label called Hidden Beach Records.

Jill Scott

Photo: Haley Madden, Redferns Music Picture Library

Dirty Samples

A sample that is recorded onto a Hip-Hop song has traditionally consisted of music grooves that were looped in order to keep a groove for the rapper. As stated earlier, samples of individual instruments, licks, melodies, drum fills, horn stabs, and fall-offs were used as effects. Next in line came samples of ambience and racket. In the 1990s, vocal samples were used as "ole school remix" producers would use the samples for novelty effects.

The idea was to sample the recording and maintain the original integrity of the singer's voice. In order to do that and still keep the beat consistent with the groove, you had to mix, blend, time-stretch, quantize, and truncate the samples. This is a tedious and technical process that requires a professional touch. Back in the day of quick *dirty samples*, a keyboardist could take a snap-shot sample and play it nearly all the way up his/her keyboard. Each time the sample was played on an ascending key, the pitch of the voice would get higher. The higher the pitch, the more chipmunk-like the voice would sound. This was known as a cheesy or *dirty sample* in Hip-Hop.

Nowadays, this dirty sample has become a desired effect and is being used in more and more of the latest Hip-Hop songs. The end result is a camouflaged vocal sound that provides familiarity, but doesn't sound as professional as the Hip-Hop artist singing or rapping on the recording.

New School Producers

Hip-Hop producer Pharrell (Pharrell Williams) is a member and founder of the group the Neptunes. He is primarily a drummer and can be heard as the lead singer in his funk/rock group the Nerds. He was a musician and co-writer with the great Teddy Riley and contributed to his *Blackstreet* CDs. His biggest hit as of today is "Drop It Like It's Hot" by Snoop Dogg. Pharrell is rapping on that song and won a GRAMMY® Award for producing it. His signature sound can be heard with the Neptunes backing Britney Spears on her song "I'm a Slave 4 You." He has a number of hits as a producer or songwriter with a myriad of Hip-Hop artists. Some artists include Wreckx-N-Effect, Kelis, (the late) Ol' Dirty Bastard and Method Man (both founding members of Wu-Tang Clan), as well as Mystikal, Britney Spears, Justin Timberlake, P Diddy, and Kanye West. He is clearly a major producer and trendsetter in Hip-Hop!

The Auto-Tune Effect

Since the demise of Milli Vanilli after the infamous record scratch incident that took place live in concert in 1990, audiences have been suspicious of lead singers in Hip-Hop. Ironically, the song they were singing when the record went bad was "Girl You Know It's True." Since some Hip-Hop singers have thin voices, it has been commonplace in the industry to auto-tune an artist who is *pitchy* (out of tune) or doesn't have a great studio-ready sound. *Auto-tuning* involves taking a voice's character and cloning it into a computer software effects processor. The vocal track is then corrected with respect to inconsistent pitches, phrasing, and diction, thus resulting into a near perfect vocal performance. When a producer does this, he smooth enhances, normalizes, and compresses the vocal to master quality on the CD.

Nowadays, the keyboard player/producer can actually play a sample of a person's lead vocal performance real-time into an audio recorder. When this occurs, it creates a computer-like facsimile of a real vocal part. In other words, it sounds like a voice being played from the keys of the keyboard player's keyboard. This is a unique sound and is used even on great singers' recordings such as Mary J. Blige's "Be Without You" or Brandy's *Full Moon*, among many others. In the 2007 release of the song "Umbrella," recorded by Rihanna and produced by Jay-Z, the lead vocal part is heavily effected by the auto-tune. This is a vivid demonstration of its striking effect. It would be advantageous for Hip-Hop artists to become acquainted with this contemporary technique.

In order to be a functional contemporary Hip-Hop keyboardist, you must be well-versed in these styles of music. However, before you can fully understand how to fuse these various styles, you must learn the structural form of Hip-Hop.

Hip-Hop Structure

Styles develop into their definitive structure as a result of a gradual continuum. Over a period of time, a style becomes coherent and its tenets can be fully observed. It has been the same for nearly all African American musical forms. Blues, gospel, jazz, R&B, and funk all had periods of time during which the style elucidated itself. This is a part of a natural progression of ideas making its way into the common musical stream. The ideas are generated from those innovators who made their mark with the listening audience. In other words, no individual can contribute to this resource of musical ideas without the general public's scrutiny and ultimate approval. That's just the way it is! In order to excel through the ranks of songwriters, artists, musicians, and producers, and influence the Hip-Hop structure, you must make hit recordings, change the rules, and stay in the game long enough to tell about it. If this happens you will be the next to shape the structure of Hip-Hop.

Structural Definitions

Intro: the beginning of the song.

Groove Section: the main groove of the song, not including its melodies or lyrics or full arrangement.

Verse One: the first full stanza of music, melody, and lyrics.

Pre Chorus: the section in which the lyrics, melodies, and rhythms change to something different, and usually builds to a musical climax.

Chorus: the main hook and melody of the song. It can contain orchestration, background vocals, or improvs in order to emphasize its thrust. It is almost always the catchy or most memorable part of the song.

Turn-a-Round: a brief musical interlude or accent devised to return to a previous section (usually the verse), or to seamlessly move on to another section.

Verse Two: the second full stanza of melody and lyrics.

Double Chorus: the same as the chorus, but played twice as long. It can contain orchestration like strings or horns to emphasize it.

Break Down: a section that usually contains a fill utilizing bass, drums, a scratch, or a squeal.

Break Beat: a section usually containing drums, rap-vocals, and percussion. It can occasionally include keyboards, guitar fills, or full background vocals, but those usually are minimal.

Stripped Rhythm: a section that only has drums and one other instrument. Although the instrument is usually bass, it can be guitar, keys, or anything. It usually occurs for no more than two bars.

Drop Out: a common drop of sound (silence) from the recording. It can be achieved by splicing on the computer or it can be performed musically. It is usually done in verses to emphasize the vocals (which remain audible), and is most commonly executed as a drum accent, but could also be completely "dead silence" from all instruments.

FX: any special effects used on the recording, including scratches, squeals, racket, hits, etc.

Chorus Tag: the end section of the song (the chorus), played over and over again with vocal improvisations.

Outro: the end of the song proper. Some songs have a set ending that is played a specific way and then completes itself.

It is important to note that these definitions refer to the style of Hip-Hop, and have slightly modified explanations when referring to other styles of music. In other words, the terminology included here should not be taken out of context.

Common Hip-Hop Song Formula

As a keyboard player, your role should be to effectively understand and execute your Hip-Hop parts. The Hip-Hop form has evolved into a basic formula, shown below.

1) **Introduction**: usually four bars, musical, rapisms, squeals, etc.

2) **Groove Section**: four-bar melody, chorus groove, rap improvisations

3) **Verse One**: eight bars with hits, vocal melody, rap, stripped rhythm

4) **Pre Chorus**: four bars with hits, vocal melody, rap, change harmony

5) **Chorus**: eight bars with hits, hook melody or rap, full rhythm, back-up vocals

6) **Turn-a-Round**: one or two bars with hits, fill pattern, rap, special FX

7) **Verse Two**: eight bars with hits, stripped rhythm, drop-out one or two bars

8) **Pre Chorus**: four bars with hits, change harmony, drop-out third bar

9) **Double Chorus**: sixteen bars with hits, hook melody, rap improvisations

10) **Break-Down**: one bar, fill, special FX, no rhythm

11) **Break Beat**: four bars with hits, hook melody, rap, back-up vocals, no rhythm

12) **Chorus Tag**: twenty-four bars with outro or fades, hook melody, rap, improvisations

The following examples represent patterns that would be found in modern Hip-Hop songs. They include all of the characteristics explored in previous chapters of this book. Keep in mind that the structure will include influences of some of the aforementioned styles and artists. You may want to preview some songs that these artists have recorded. You can stream from the web or even download free samples of snippets of songs. While listening, see if you can pick up the structure and follow along. You are encouraged to listen often and learn about this music if you intend to perform it professionally.

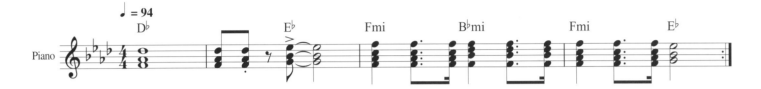

Wedding Regrets

TRACK 70

In "Call Me Okay?", the groove is primarily in 4/4 time, but could be interpreted in 6/4, or even in multiples of 2/4. This pattern, although notated in common time, is hinting at polyrhythm. Listen for the variety of rhythms in the drum part, the guitar part, and the keyboard part. This type of interplay is common in the Hip-Hop songs of artists like E-40, Usher, Floetry, and more.

Call Me Okay?

TRACK 71

Multi-syncopation is present within the drum, bass, and guitar parts in "Dirty South." This is what is known as polyrhythm. Listen for the dynamic swell on the synthesizer part. You can use your modulation wheel or slide ribbon to get this effect.

Hell 2 Da Yeah!

St. Louis

TRACK 76

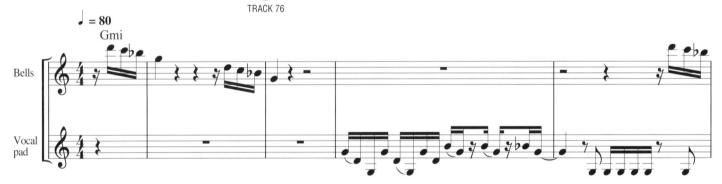

Lolly Pop Love

TRACK 77

In "Lean Pork Shoulder," the pulse is felt in half time, even though it is written and counted in double time. This is another interpretation of polyrhythm. Listen to the multi-layered keyboard parts. This kind of effect is very common in the songs of Gangsta rap and Hip-Hop artists like E-40, Too Short, Snoop Dogg, Kurupt, T-Pain, and others. Many Hip-Hop producers are returning to the very heavy analog sound of synthesizers used during the 1980s. Using the right sound for this kind of Hip-Hop goes a long way toward playing with authority.

Lean Pork Shoulder

TRACK 78

Yes Suh

TRACK 79

Bonus Tracks

The following examples are using the metric displacement feel mentioned in Chapter 9. Be careful to keep good time and be sure not to rush through this exaggerated feel. Have fun and good luck!

Solangello

TRACK 80

Chuckie

TRACK 81

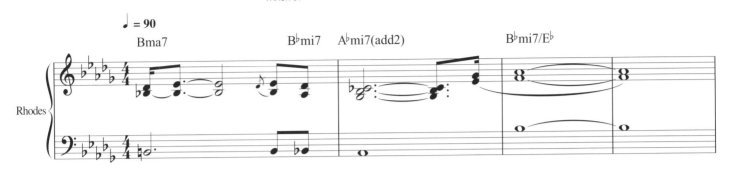

Lonely Cuz

TRACK 82

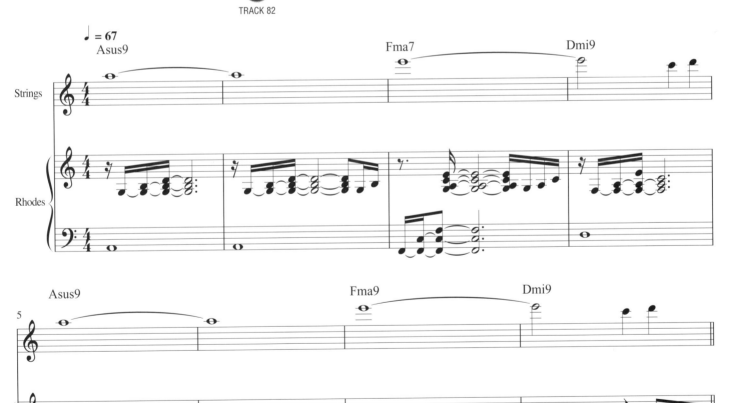

Neo Soleh
TRACK 83

Ya Feel Me?
TRACK 84

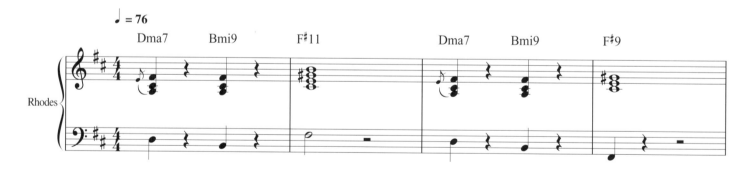

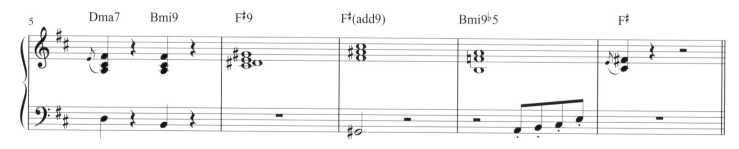

Fire Place

TRACK 85

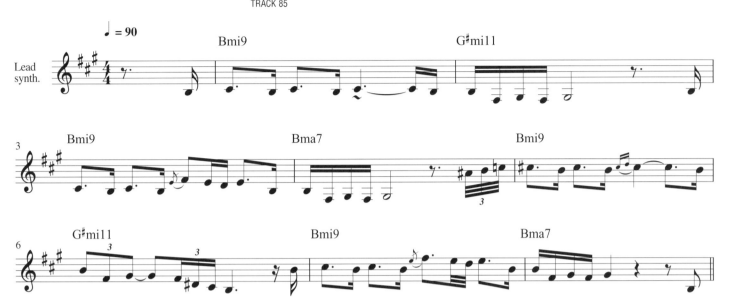

Creepin

TRACK 86

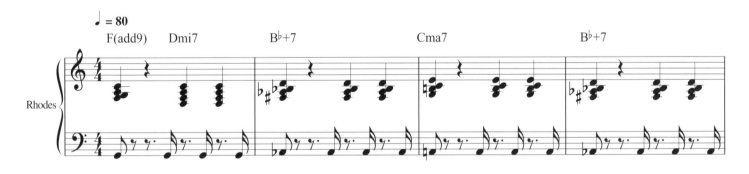

Reference Guide

The following information has been provided for those interested in further studies and understanding of the music, culture, and personalities within the world of Hip-Hop. Obviously, there are works currently in production that will continue to bring this information forward. This style of music is always evolving, so look to the artists themselves to help show you the way to the future.

You should listen to all of the works of the many artists mentioned in this book. You are also encouraged to listen to your favorite artists and try to emulate the music that you hear on the recordings, including the production techniques. And don't forget to try your hand at rapping! Remember, rappers are the center of Hip-Hop, so it wouldn't be a bad idea to go to "free-style" live performances, poetry readings, spoken word events, and rap concerts to watch other rappers, live musicians, and DJs do their thing. Books, videos, DVDs, and newspaper and magazine articles are also very good ways to learn.

Publications

Can't Stop Won't Stop by Jeff Chang

The Hip-Hop Years: A History of Rap by Alex Ogg and David Upshal

The Vibe History of Hip-Hop by Alan Light

Hip-Hop America by Nelson George

Move the Crowd: Voices and Faces of the Hip-Hop Nation by Gregor and Dimitri Ehrlich

Yes, Yes Ya'll by Jim Fricke

Biography – Tupac Shakur (1971-1996), sketch by Simon Glickman

Rap Attack 2 by David Toop

King of Rock by Darryl McDaniels (DMC) and Bruce Haring

United States vs. Hip-Hop by Julian L.D. Shabazz

Listen Up! Spoken Word Poetry by Zoe Anglesey

Last Night a DJ Saved My Life by Bill Brewster & Frank Broughton

Life and Def: Sex, Drugs, Money + God by Russell Simmons with Nelson George

Back in the Days by Jamel Shabazz

Instructional CDs and DVDs

The Commandments of R&B Drummimg, DVD by Zoro

Record Industry 411, CD by Lonzo Williams

Word in Motion, DVD

Hip-Hop You Don't Stop, DVD and CD

The Roots of Rap CD: Rap from the '20s and '30s

Prosample: Hip-Hop Samples CDs Vol. 1-5

Dirty South Hip-Hop Sample CD Vol. 49

LA Riot Hip-Hop & Rap Samples Vol. 1&2

The Poetics of Hip-Hop, CD/DVD

Off Da Hook, Video Series, VHS & DVD

Jam Master Jay, DJ DVD

Live Concert Events and Movies

The Show (Tripp Loce, Dr. Dre, Russell Simmons, The Notorious B.I.G.)

Rudy Ray Moore Biography

Jay-Z Fade 2 Black Live

Fear of a Black Hat

Hip-Hop All Stars

Hip-Hop Story 1, 2, & 3

Blackalicious Live in Seattle

50 Cent Live

Eminem: Anger Management Live

8 Mile

Death Row Uncut

Up in Smoke Tour

Dave Chappelle's Block Party

Trina Live & Uncut

The Roots Live

Tupac Shakur: Complete Live and House of Blues

OutKast Dare to Be Different

E-40

Usher Live

Hip-Hop Nation 1–6

Bone Thugs-N-Harmony: Live & Uncut

Ludacris Red Light District

Snoop Dogg Diary of a Pimp

Wild Style

Web Sites

hiphopportal.com

MTV.com

cantstopwontstop.com

daveyd.com

BET.com

hiphopsite.com

hiphop-directory.com

KEYBOARD STYLE SERIES

THE COMPLETE GUIDE WITH CD!

These book/CD packs provide focused lessons that contain valuable how-to insight, essential playing tips, and beneficial information for all players. From comping to soloing, comprehensive treatment is given to each subject. The companion CD features many of the examples in the book performed either solo or with a full band.

BEBOP JAZZ PIANO
by John Valerio

This book provides detailed information for bebop and jazz keyboardists on: chords and voicings, harmony and chord progressions, scales and tonality, common melodic figures and patterns, comping, characteristic tunes, the styles of Bud Powell and Thelonious Monk, and more. Includes 5 combo performances at the end of the book.
00290535 Book/CD Pack......................................$18.95

BLUES PIANO
by Mark Harrison

With this book/CD pack, you'll learn the theory, the tools, and even the tricks that the pros use to play the blues. You also get seven complete tunes to jam with on the CD. Covers: scales and chords; left-hand patterns; walking bass; endings and turnarounds; right-hand techniques; how to solo with blues scales; crossover licks; and more.
00311007 Book/CD Pack......................................$17.95

COUNTRY PIANO
by Mark Harrison

Learn the theory, the tools, and the tricks used by the pros to get that authentic country sound. This book/CD pack covers: scales and chords, walkup and walkdown patterns, comping in traditional and modern country, Nashville "fretted piano" techniques and more. At the end, you'll get to jam along with seven complete tunes.
00311052 Book/CD Pack......................................$17.95

POST-BOP JAZZ PIANO
by John Valerio

This book/CD pack will teach you the basic skills needed to play post-bop jazz piano. Learn the theory, the tools, and the tricks used by the pros to play in the style of Bill Evans, Thelonious Monk, Herbie Hancock, McCoy Tyner, Chick Corea and others. Topics covered include: chord voicings, scales and tonality, modality, and more.
00311005 Book/CD Pack......................................$17.95

R&B KEYBOARD
by Mark Harrison

From soul to funk to disco to pop, you'll learn the theory, the tools, and the tricks used by the pros with this book/CD pack. Topics covered include: scales and chords, harmony and voicings, progressions and comping, rhythmic concepts, characteristic stylings, the development of R&B, and more! Includes seven songs.
00310881 Book/CD Pack......................................$17.95

ROCK KEYBOARD
by Scott Miller

Learn to comp or solo in any of your favorite rock styles. Listen to the CD to hear your parts fit in with the total groove of the band. Includes 99 tracks! Covers: classic rock, pop/rock, blues rock, Southern rock, hard rock, progressive rock, alternative rock and heavy metal.
00310823 Book/CD Pack......................................$17.95

ROCK 'N' ROLL PIANO
by Andy Vinter

Take your place alongside Fats Domino, Jerry Lee Lewis, Little Richard, and other legendary players of the '50s and '60s! This book/CD pack covers: left-hand patterns; basic rock 'n' roll progressions; right-hand techniques; straight eighths vs. swing eighths; glisses, crushed notes, rolls, note clusters and more. Includes six complete tunes.
00310912 Book/CD Pack......................................$17.95

SMOOTH JAZZ PIANO
by Mark Harrison

Learn the skills you need to play smooth jazz piano – the theory, the tools, and the tricks used by the pros. Topics covered include: scales and chords; harmony and voicings; progressions and comping; rhythmic concepts; melodies and soloing; characteristic stylings; discussions on jazz evolution.
00311095 Book/CD Pack......................................$17.95

STRIDE & SWING PIANO
by John Valerio

Learn the styles of the stride and swing piano masters, such as Scott Joplin, Jimmy Yancey, Pete Johnson, Jelly Roll Morton, James P. Johnson, Fats Waller, Teddy Wilson, and Art Tatum. This book/CD pack covers classic ragtime, early blues and boogie woogie, New Orleans jazz and more. Includes 14 songs.
00310882 Book/CD Pack......................................$17.95

Prices, contents, and availability
subject to change without notice.

The Keyboard Play-Along series will help you quickly and easily play your favorite songs as played by your favorite artists. Just follow the music in the book, listen to the CD to hear how the keyboard should sound, and then play along using the separate backing tracks. The melody and lyrics are also included in the book in case you want to sing, or simply to help you follow along. The audio CD is playable on any CD player. For PC and Mac users, the CD is enhanced so you can adjust the recording to any tempo without changing pitch! Each book/CD pack in this series features eight great songs.

1. POP/ROCK HITS

Against All Odds (Take a Look at Me Now) (Phil Collins) • Deacon Blues (Steely Dan) • (Everything I Do) I Do It for You (Bryan Adams) • Hard to Say I'm Sorry (Chicago) • Kiss on My List (Hall & Oates) • My Life (Billy Joel) • Walking in Memphis (Marc Cohn) • What a Fool Believes (The Doobie Brothers).
00699875 Keyboard Transcriptions..$14.95

2. SOFT ROCK

Don't Know Much (Aaron Neville) • Glory of Love (Peter Cetera) • I Write the Songs (Barry Manilow) • It's Too Late (Carole King) • Just Once (James Ingram) • Making Love Out of Nothing at All (Air Supply) • We've Only Just Begun (Carpenters) • You Are the Sunshine of My Life (Stevie Wonder).
00699876 Keyboard Transcriptions..$12.95

3. CLASSIC ROCK

Against the Wind (Bob Seger) • Come Sail Away (Styx) • Don't Do Me like That (Tom Petty and the Heartbreakers) • Jessica (Allman Brothers) • Say You Love Me (Fleetwood Mac) • Takin' Care of Business (Bachman-Turner Overdrive) • Werewolves of London (Warren Zevon) • You're My Best Friend (Queen).
00699877 Keyboard Transcriptions..$14.95

4. CONTEMPORARY ROCK

Angel (Sarah McLachlan) • Beautiful (Christina Aguilera) • Because of You (Kelly Clarkson) • Don't Know Why (Norah Jones) • Fallin' (Alicia Keys) • Listen to Your Heart (D.H.T.) • A Thousand Miles (Vanessa Carlton) • Unfaithful (Rihanna).
00699878 Keyboard Transcriptions..$12.95

5. ROCK HITS

Back at One (Brian McKnight) • Brick (Ben Folds) • Clocks (Coldplay) • Drops of Jupiter (Tell Me) (Train) • Home (Michael Buble) • 100 Years (Five for Fighting) • This Love (Maroon 5) • You're Beautiful (James Blunt)
00699879 Keyboard Transcriptions..$14.95

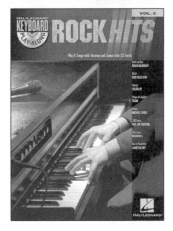

6. ROCK BALLADS

Bridge over Troubled Water (Simon & Garfunkel) • Easy (Commodores) • Hey Jude (Beatles) • Imagine (John Lennon) • Maybe I'm Amazed (Paul McCartney) • A Whiter Shade of Pale (Procol Harum) • You Are So Beautiful (Joe Cocker) • Your Song (Elton John).
00699880 Keyboard Transcriptions..$14.95

More Volumes Coming Soon, Including:
Vol. 7 Rock Classics

FOR MORE INFORMATION,
SEE YOUR LOCAL MUSIC DEALER,
OR WRITE TO:

HAL•LEONARD®
CORPORATION
7777 W. BLUEMOUND RD. P.O. BOX 13819
MILWAUKEE, WISCONSIN 53213

Visit Hal Leonard Online at **www.halleonard.com**

Prices, contents, and availability subject to change without notice.

NOTE-FOR-NOTE KEYBOARD TRANSCRIPTIONS

These outstanding collections feature note-for-note transcriptions from the artists who made the songs famous.
No matter what style you play, these books are perfect for performers or students who want to play just like their keyboard idols.

ACOUSTIC PIANO BALLADS

16 acoustic piano favorites: Angel • Candle in the Wind • Don't Let the Sun Go Down on Me • Endless Love • Imagine • It's Too Late • Let It Be • Mandy • Ribbon in the Sky • Sailing • She's Got a Way • So Far Away • Tapestry • You Never Give Me Your Money • You've Got a Friend • Your Song.

00690351 / $19.95

ELTON JOHN

18 of Elton John's best songs: Bennie and the Jets • Candle in the Wind • Crocodile Rock • Daniel • Don't Let the Sun Go Down on Me • Goodbye Yellow Brick Road • I Guess That's Why They Call It the Blues • Little Jeannie • Rocket Man • Your Song • and more!

00694829 / $20.95

THE BEATLES KEYBOARD BOOK

23 Beatles favorites, including: All You Need Is Love • Back in the U.S.S.R. • Come Together • Get Back • Good Day Sunshine • Hey Jude • Lady Madonna • Let It Be • Lucy in the Sky with Diamonds • Ob-La-Di, Ob-La-Da • Oh! Darling • Penny Lane • Revolution • We Can Work It Out • With a Little Help from My Friends • and more.

00694827 / $20.95

THE CAROLE KING KEYBOARD BOOK

16 of King's greatest songs: Beautiful • Been to Canaan • Home Again • I Feel the Earth Move • It's Too Late • Jazzman • (You Make Me Feel) Like a Natural Woman • Nightingale • Smackwater Jack • So Far Away • Sweet Seasons • Tapestry • Way Over Yonder • Where You Lead • Will You Love Me Tomorrow • You've Got a Friend.

00690554 / $19.95

CLASSIC ROCK

35 all-time rock classics: Beth • Bloody Well Right • Changes • Cold as Ice • Come Sail Away • Don't Do Me like That • Hard to Handle • Heaven • Killer Queen • King of Pain • Layla • Light My Fire • Oye Como Va • Piano Man • Takin' Care of Business • Werewolves of London • and more.

00310940 / $24.95

POP/ROCK

35 songs, including: Africa • Against All Odds • Axel F • Centerfold • Chariots of Fire • Cherish • Don't Let the Sun Go Down on Me • Drops of Jupiter (Tell Me) • Faithfully • It's Too Late • Just the Way You Are • Let It Be • Mandy • Sailing • Sweet Dreams Are Made of This • Walking in Memphis • and more.

00310939 / $24.95

JAZZ

24 favorites from Bill Evans, Thelonious Monk, Oscar Peterson, Bud Powell, Art Tatum and more. Includes: Ain't Misbehavin' • April in Paris • Autumn in New York • Body and Soul • Freddie Freeloader • Giant Steps • My Funny Valentine • Satin Doll • Song for My Father • Stella by Starlight • and more.

00310941 / $22.95

R&B

35 R&B classics: Baby Love • Boogie on Reggae Woman • Easy • Endless Love • Fallin' • Green Onions • Higher Ground • I'll Be There • Just Once • Money (That's What I Want) • On the Wings of Love • Ribbon in the Sky • This Masquerade • Three Times a Lady • and more.

00310942 / $24.95

THE BILLY JOEL KEYBOARD BOOK

16 mega-hits from the Piano Man himself: Allentown • And So It Goes • Honesty • Just the Way You Are • Movin' Out • My Life • New York State of Mind • Piano Man • Pressure • She's Got a Way • Tell Her About It • and more.

00694828 / $22.95

STEVIE WONDER

14 of Stevie's most popular songs: Boogie on Reggae Woman • Hey Love • Higher Ground • I Wish • Isn't She Lovely • Lately • Living for the City • Overjoyed • Ribbon in the Sky • Send One Your Love • Superstition • That Girl • You Are the Sunshine of My Life • You Haven't Done Nothin'.

00306698 / $21.95

Prices, contents and availability subject to change without notice.

FOR MORE INFORMATION, SEE YOUR LOCAL MUSIC DEALER,
OR WRITE TO:

HAL•LEONARD®
CORPORATION
7777 W. BLUEMOUND RD. P.O. BOX 13819 MILWAUKEE, WI 53213

Visit Hal Leonard online at www.halleonard.com

0107

KEYBOARD *signature licks*

These exceptional book/CD packs teach keyboardists the techniques and styles used by popular artists from yesterday and today. Each folio breaks down the trademark riffs and licks used by these great performers.

BEST OF BEBOP PIANO
by Gene Rizzo

16 bebop piano transcriptions: April in Paris • Between the Devil and the Deep Blue Sea • I Don't Stand a Ghost of a Chance • If I Were a Bell • Lullaby of Birdland • On a Clear Day (You Can See Forever) • Satin Doll • Thou Swell • and more.
00695734...$19.95

CONTEMPORARY CHRISTIAN
by Todd Lowry

Learn the trademark keyboard styles and techniques of today's top contemporary Christian artists. 12 songs, including: Fool for You (Nichole Nordeman) • The Great Divide (Point of Grace) • His Strength Is Perfect (Steven Curtis Chapman) • How Beautiful (Twila Paris) • If I Stand (Rich Mullins) • Know You in the Now (Michael Card) • and more.
00695753...$19.95

BILL EVANS
by Brent Edstrom

12 songs from pianist Bill Evans, including: Five • One for Helen • The Opener • Peace Piece • Peri's Scope • Quiet Now • Re: Person I Knew • Time Remembered • Turn Out the Stars • Very Early • Waltz for Debby • 34 Skidoo.
00695714...$22.95

BEN FOLDS FIVE
by Todd Lowry

16 songs from four Ben Folds Five albums: Alice Childress • Battle of Who Could Care Less • Boxing • Brick • Don't Change Your Plans • Evaporated • Kate • The Last Polka • Lullabye • Magic • Narcolepsy • Philosophy • Song for the Dumped • Underground.
00695578...$22.95

BILLY JOEL CLASSICS: 1974-1980
by Robbie Gennet

15 popular hits from the '70s by Billy Joel: Big Shot • Captain Jack • Don't Ask Me Why • The Entertainer • Honesty • Just the Way You Are • Movin' Out (Anthony's Song) • My Life • New York State of Mind • Piano Man • Root Beer Rag • Say Goodbye to Hollywood • Scenes from an Italian Restaurant • She's Always a Woman • The Stranger.
00695581...$22.95

BILLY JOEL HITS: 1981-1993
by Todd Lowry

15 more hits from Billy Joel in the '80s and '90s: All About Soul • Allentown • And So It Goes • Baby Grand • I Go to Extremes • Leningrad • Lullabye (Goodnight, My Angel) • Modern Woman • Pressure • The River of Dreams • She's Got a Way • Tell Her About It • This Is the Time • Uptown Girl • You're Only Human (Second Wind).
00695582...$22.95

ELTON JOHN CLASSIC HITS
by Todd Lowry

10 of Elton's best are presented in this book/CD pack: Blue Eyes • Chloe • Don't Go Breaking My Heart • Don't Let the Sun Go Down on Me • Ego • I Guess That's Why They Call It the Blues • Little Jeannie • Sad Songs (Say So Much) • Someone Saved My Life Tonight • Sorry Seems to Be the Hardest Word.
00695688...$22.95

LENNON & MCCARTNEY HITS
by Todd Lowry

Features 15 hits from A-L for keyboard by the legendary songwriting team of John Lennon and Paul McCartney. Songs include: All You Need Is Love • Back in the U.S.S.R. • The Ballad of John and Yoko • Because • Birthday • Come Together • A Day in the Life • Don't Let Me Down • Drive My Car • Get Back • Good Day Sunshine • Hello, Goodbye • Hey Jude • In My Life • Lady Madonna.
00695650...$22.95

LENNON & MCCARTNEY FAVORITES
by Todd Lowry

16 more hits (L-Z) from The Beatles: Let It Be • The Long and Winding Road • Lucy in the Sky with Diamonds • Martha My Dear • Ob-La-Di, Ob-La-Da • Oh! Darling • Penny Lane • Revolution 9 • Rocky Raccoon • She's a Woman • Strawberry Fields Forever • We Can Work It Out • With a Little Help from My Friends • The Word • You're Going to Lose That Girl • Your Mother Should Know.
00695651...$22.95

BEST OF ROCK
by Todd Lowry

12 songs are analyzed: Bloody Well Right (Supertramp) • Cold as Ice (Foreigner) • Don't Do Me Like That (Tom Petty & The Heartbreakers) • Don't Let the Sun Go Down on Me (Elton John) • I'd Do Anything for Love (Meat Loaf) • Killer Queen (Queen) • Lady Madonna (The Beatles) • Light My Fire (The Doors) • Piano Man (Billy Joel) • Point of No Return (Kansas) • Separate Ways (Journey) • Werewolves of London (Warren Zevon).
00695751...$19.95

BEST OF ROCK 'N' ROLL PIANO
by David Bennett Cohen

12 of the best hits for piano are presented in this pack. Songs include: At the Hop • Blueberry Hill • Brown-Eyed Handsome Man • Charlie Brown • Great Balls of Fire • Jailhouse Rock • Lucille • Rock and Roll Is Here to Stay • Runaway • Tutti Frutti • Yakety Yak • You Never Can Tell.
00695627...$19.95

BEST OF STEVIE WONDER
by Todd Lowry

This book/CD pack includes musical examples, lessons, biographical notes, and more for 14 of Stevie Wonder's best songs. Features: I Just Called to Say I Love You • My Cherie Amour • Part Time Lover • Sir Duke • Superstition • You Are the Sunshine of My Life • and more.
00695605...$22.95

0304

MORE BOOKS FROM

⌐HAL•LEONARD®

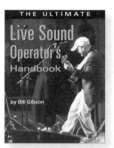

HOME STUDIO CLINIC

A MUSICIAN'S GUIDE TO PROFESSIONAL RECORDING

by Emile Menasché

Written from a musician's point of view, this book is designed to help you build and use a studio based on your musical goals. By exploring concepts and various common tasks, this reader-friendly book gives you the know-how to choose equipment that suits your needs and style, and the techniques to use it effectively.

_____00331466..$24.95
(ISBN 1-4234-1807-7) (UPC 8-84088-10349-1)

THE ULTIMATE LIVE SOUND OPERATOR'S HANDBOOK 📀DVD

by Bill Gibson

High-quality audio is imperative, whether you're running sound for a rock, country, punk, or jazz band performing in clubs, arenas, or outdoor parks. This comprehensive handbook focuses on each aspect of live sound in a way that is easy to understand, breaking the process down into principles and practices that assist the modern sound tech in everything from planning and budgeting to mixing and recording the live show.

_____00331469..$34.95
(ISBN 1-4234-1971-5) (UPC 8-84088-10676-8)

101 RECORDING TIPS

STUFF ALL THE PROS KNOW AND USE

by Adam St. James

Book/CD Pack

Tips, suggestions, advice, and other useful information garnered through a lifetime of home and pro studio recording adventures. It's an essential collection of tricks of the trade that will improve anyone's home or pro studio recordings. The accompanying CD includes nearly one hour of audio demonstrations.

_____00311035..$14.95
(ISBN 0-634-06562-9) (UPC 0-73999-86774-9)

ALL ABOUT HARD DISK RECORDERS

AN INTRODUCTION TO THE CREATIVE WORLD OF DIGITAL, HARD DISK RECORDING

by Robby Berman

This book takes you from the very beginning with an overview, to practical tips for taking advantage of the choices you have with this flexible recording system. Topics include: setting up a hard drive; principles of audio editing; maintaining a hard drive; how a work station operates; and more.

_____00331033..$19.95
(ISBN 0-634-05734-0) (UPC 0-73999-60832-8)

ALL ABOUT MUSIC TECHNOLOGY IN WORSHIP

HOW TO SET UP AND PLAN A MUSICAL PERFORMANCE

by Steve Young

edited by Corey Fournier

Church musicians today must possess a working knowledge of music technology to offer their music ministry in the varied and demanding settings of worship. This book provides simple instructions on everything from synthesizers, MIDI, and sequencing to percussion, bass, and guitar technology.

_____00331034..$19.95
(ISBN 0-634-05449-X) (UPC 0-73999-54088-8)

THE BASICS OF LIVE SOUND

TIPS, TECHNIQUES & LUCKY GUESSES

by Jerry J. Slone

This beginner's guide provides easy-to-understand coverage aimed at the novice on topics such as: sound and hearing; microphone models, specs, and techniques; mixers; equalization; amplifiers; speakers; the audio chain; schools and universities for continuing education; and more.

_____00330779..$9.95
(ISBN 0-634-03028-0) (UPC 0-73999-30779-5)

THE DESKTOP STUDIO

by Emile Menasché

With the right software, your computer can be a recorder, mixer, editor, video production system, and even a musical instrument. *The Desktop Studio* will help you get the most out of your computer and turn it – and you – into a creative powerhouse. It is a fully illustrated, comprehensive look at software and hardware, and provides expert tips for getting the most out of your music computer.

_____00330783..$22.95
(ISBN 0-634-03019-1) (UPC 0-73999-65680-0)

LIVE SOUND FOR MUSICIANS

by Rudy Trubitt

Live Sound for Musicians shows you how to keep your band's PA system working smoothly, from set-up and soundcheck right through your performance. If you're the person in the band who runs the PA, this is the book you've been waiting for!

_____00330249..$19.95
(ISBN 0-7935-6852-8) (UPC 0-73999-79303-1)

SONIC ALCHEMY

VISIONARY MUSIC PRODUCERS AND THEIR MAVERICK RECORDINGS

by David N. Howard

You may not have heard of them, but you have certainly heard their songs! From the lo-fidelity origins of early pioneers to today's dazzling technocrats, this book explores the influence of these visionary music producers through popular music and the crucial role they have played in shaping the way we hear music today.

_____00331051..$18.95
(ISBN 0-634-05560-7) (UPC 0-73999-77098-8)

CHURCH SOUND SYSTEMS

by Lonnie Park

This easy-to-understand book is for everyone involved with church sound. Whether you want to design a new system or get the most out of the one you have, this handy guide will help you let your message be heard! It covers everything you need to know about: design and layout of your sound system; choosing the right microphones; speaker setup and positioning; mixers; and much more.

_____00330542..$12.95
(ISBN 0-634-01782-9) (UPC 0-73999-23923-2)

FOR MORE INFORMATION, SEE YOUR LOCAL MUSIC DEALER,
OR WRITE TO:

⌐HAL•LEONARD®
CORPORATION
7777 W. BLUEMOUND RD. P.O. BOX 13819 MILWAUKEE, WI 53213